# We
## Talk of
# Christ
## We Rejoice
### in
# Christ

# NEAL A. MAXWELL

# We Talk of Christ

# We Rejoice in Christ

DESERET BOOK
Salt Lake City, Utah

To Colleen for her usual intuitive insights and helpful reactions but most of all for her constant, Christian example.

ISBN 0-87747-762-0
Library of Congress Catalog Card Number 84-71873

First printing September 1984

# Contents

# Acknowledgments

My gratitude goes to those who have helped so much with their reactions to the first-draft manuscript—Elizabeth Haglund, Jeffrey Holland, Roy W. Doxey, and Daniel H. Ludlow; my special appreciation for their insights and encouragement.

My thanks also to Ronald Millet for his support and to Eleanor Knowles and Jack Lyon for their subsequent excellent editorial assistance.

Appreciation is clearly due and gladly given to Susan Jackson for her patient processing of words and changes.

# *Introduction*

For the limitations inherent in this volume as well as the views expressed herein the author alone is responsible. This is *not* an official Church publication.

The purposes of this volume are clearly not literary. It was written to spread the glorious and desperately needed gospel truths and doctrines pertaining to Jesus Christ, our Savior, upon Whom all else that really matters finally depends. He and His atoning sacrifice are the operating center of our Father's plan of salvation, and if we would be truly happy, He must be the operating center of our lives.

Faith in the Lord Jesus Christ is, after all, the *first* principle of His gospel; when it is not in place, little else that matters can be done. With genuine faith, however, so much can be done.

Yet some of us live, most of the time, astonishingly below our individual and collective possibilities. This shortfall usually occurs because individual faith is hardly faith, because it is soft instead of firm, uninformed instead of knowledgeable, and superficial instead of deeply rooted.

This book presents its message through characters engaged in group gospel discussion in order to demonstrate a range of comments, convictions, and concerns pertaining to faith in the Lord Jesus Christ and in our Heavenly Father's plan of salvation for mankind.

Though the conversation and communicants in this

volume are fictitious, the issues and truths discussed are very real and also very important. To portray these issues and truths, the individuals in this book are of necessity somewhat atypical. They are especially—though not equally—conversant and knowledgeable concerning the gospel. Furthermore, they are genuinely and "anxiously engaged" in deepening their discipleship.

However, they have some conversational moments wherein they "talk of Christ" simply to "rejoice in Christ." These moments permit them to explore and to enjoy their faith as well as defend it.

There are some moments, too, when it proves more important for one of them to say something than it is for the others to hear what is said. The conversations portrayed leave some topical strands untied and some matters unexplored or unevenly explored.

The characters are:

Noel, husband and father, true believer* in Jesus Christ and His latter-day prophets, and professor of chemistry.

Rachel, wife and mother, true believer in Jesus Christ and His latter-day prophets, and former high school teacher.

Jeffrey, husband and father, true believer in Jesus Christ and His latter-day prophets, and businessman and investment counselor.

Pauline, wife and mother, true believer in Jesus Christ and His latter-day prophets, and early-morning seminary teacher.

Winston, father, recent widower, rapidly emerging true believer in Jesus Christ and His latter-day prophets, and government official.

Charles, divorced father, one truly seeking to become a true believer in Jesus Christ and His latter-day prophets, and professor of languages.

The conversations occur over a period of months and usually involve all of the characters in a gospel study group. Because of their close friendships and their earnest pursuit of discipleship, most of their conversations ensue not only by appointment as to place and time but also after each person has been asked to come prepared on a particular gospel topic. A "lesson" is presented by one or more of the participants with reaction and discussion by the group.

Noel is the informal leader of the group, but others make presentations. Charles, being somewhat less settled, tends to raise issues and concerns but in genuine spiritual inquiry.

---

*The designation *true believer* was used by Nephi (4 Nephi 1:36, 37) centuries before Eric Hoffer's pejorative use of the phrase. Long ago it meant "a band of Christians" who "gladly" took upon themselves the name of Christ. (Alma 46:13-15.) The six portrayed in this volume are such a band, too.

# First Conversation: Faith and Knowledge

"And now, behold, is your knowledge
perfect? Yea, your knowledge is perfect in that
thing, and your faith is dormant; and this
because you know."
(Alma 32:34.)

*The setting: An autumn Sunday evening in Noel and Rachel's living room. A lively gospel discussion is in progress. All six friends are present. The topic is faith—not vague, generalized faith, but particularized faith, which is based upon partial knowledge and which can bring further knowledge.*

———————

NOEL: It's good to meet with you all tonight. Alma's brilliant chapter on the nature of faith will be our focus, and we will particularly examine a prepositional phrase therein. Note how Alma wrote that faith in a particular gospel principle can become knowledge "in that thing." (Alma 32:34.) This is much more than a somewhat awkward three-word prepositional phrase that might have been rendered "in that matter" or "in that regard." In any event, it is a useful key to understanding the nature of faith, inasmuch as it calls to our attention the incremental, individual verification process by which we can move from a desire to believe, to belief, to faith, and finally to knowledge. By experimenting with each individual gospel truth, we can, over time, come to know, by personal experience, of its truth.

RACHEL: Frankly, before Noel and I began to prepare this lesson, while we'd thought of how our faith can grow incrementally, we'd thought less about how faith in Jesus Christ is to be accompanied by faith in each of the truths and principles of His gospel—and, furthermore, in the overall plan of salvation.

NOEL: Nephi wrote that we "have not come thus far," that is, entering the straight and narrow path, except "by the word of Christ with unshaken faith in him." Neither can we *stay* on it in any other way. (2 Nephi 31:19.)

RACHEL: And our staying power is greater as we verify the gospel, principle by principle, if we do not lose sight of the overall plan of salvation. A sister said in Relief Society last Sunday that she could more easily carry the "cross daily" if her focus is kept on eternity. (Luke 9:23.)

JEFFREY: But faith in the Father and His Son Jesus Christ is the first principle of the gospel, isn't it? Following the first principle is surely necessary to the full keeping of the first great commandment.

NOEL: Yes, but being in the midst of the pressures of the business world, as you are, Jeffrey, without an overall focus—not only on Jesus, but on His Father's plan—would diffuse and dilute the meaning and purpose of life for you.

JEFFREY: True. The cares of the world are so easy to care about!

PAULINE: I agree with what is being said about faith being specific but also broad. For instance, faith in the plan of salvation is so essential to the serious keeping of the second great commandment. Otherwise we could see others merely as functions instead of everlasting entities.

NOEL: So true. Without faith in the Father and Son, without getting outside oneself to love, how realistic is it to think in terms of loving one's neighbor?

WINSTON: More to the point, without verification of the meaning and purposes of life, why behave? Why be good? Why pay attention to, let alone love, one's neighbor? I think it was Max Weber who coined the phrase "hedonists without hearts."[1]

If there is no *raison d'etre*, there's little reason to care and to love. But when one sees and accepts the purpose and meaning of life, as God has given it to us in the gospel of His Son, then, hard as it is, one can be much more serious about keeping the second commandment.

NOEL: If my memory serves me correctly, Paul wrote that "without faith it is impossible to please [God]."

(Hebrews 11:6.) In such a setting as we are now stress-
ing, faith is not arbitrary but a salutary requirement
from God.

CHARLES: No wonder Teresa of Avila said that life
without knowing God is no more than a night in a
second-class hotel![2]

NOEL: While rereading, as you all no doubt did, the
thirty-second chapter of Alma, I was also reminded
that faith is not perfect knowledge. Yet the adjective
"perfect" suggests to me that some knowledge may
still be present, but not perfect knowledge, for that
would take us beyond the realm of faith. We can, however, have layers upon layers of knowledge reflecting
positive, past experiences in trusting God. Each of
these should help us to trust afresh now.

CHARLES: But this is still not a perfect knowledge concerning our *present* circumstances or challenges, is it,
Noel?

NOEL: No. "Perfect knowledge" in the broadest sense
would presumably not be achieved until the perfect
day. Until we enter the presence of the Father and the
Son. Until we get back our memories of the first estate.
But, meanwhile, faith can move on to knowledge in
which something is repeatedly and demonstrably
proved to be true. For instance, listen to this passage
from the Doctrine and Covenants: "When the Savior
shall appear we shall see him as he is. We shall see that
he is a man like ourselves. And that same sociality
which exists among us here will exist among us there,
only it will be coupled with eternal glory, which glory
we do not now enjoy." (D&C 130:1, 2.)

RACHEL: You're saying that we can actually come to

know well, before that special moment, however, that God loves us individually and perfectly, that prayers are answered, that forgiveness brings great joy and is a true and correct principle?

NOEL: Yes, I am. Furthermore, the verifiable truths comprise such a long list . . .

JEFFREY: The past can provide compelling incentives for the present to go on trusting and believing in God. After all, don't we sing about how "we've proved him in days that are past"?[3]

PAULINE: Yet, Noel, as you have demonstrated with regard to three words of Alma, we also sometimes slide so quickly over still other evocative words of Alma. He stated that experimenting on the gospel requires an *arousing* of our "faculties," anything but a passive act! (Alma 32:27.) These words suggest a genuine commitment to the experiment, not merely a casual or half-hearted "wait-and-see" attitude.

NOEL: Then, Pauline, as we experiment with different truths of the gospel, line upon line, precept by precept, experience by experience, we learn that the gospel really works in one thing after another. (See Isaiah 28:10, 13.)

CHARLES: As I ponder the cumulative commitment about which you're speaking, I recall that Moses led a people who witnessed many miracles. Yet as new tests came, his people apparently lacked fresh faith. What does that say for cumulative commitment?

NOEL: They did falter, Charles! In fact, note this wording in Deuteronomy: "Yet *in this thing* ye did not believe the Lord your God." (Deuteronomy 1:32, italics added.) Worse still, the children of Israel on one occasion even talked of designating a leader to take them back to Egypt. (See Numbers 14:4.)

It seems, in retrospect, that ancient Israel failed to understand their God and His purposes. By the way, in the 3rd Lecture on Faith—and these lectures were prepared under Joseph Smith's direction—we read that one of the three essentials necessary to faith is "a correct idea of [God's] character, perfections, and attributes."[4] A matter of no small importance to the building of our faith.

RACHEL: Not surprising, is it, that a burdened Moses wished that each and all of his people could be knowing prophets? (Numbers 11:29.)

CHARLES: Noel and Rachel, I fear that without intending to do so, you make deepening one's faith sound a little too mechanical and the progression therein a little too easy . . .

NOEL: I surely don't mean to. It is not an automatic accrual. Don't we begin to see a pattern emerge, however, in which our faith can move toward knowledge on the basis of confirming experience growing out of various incidents? These experiences constitute the special testing moment or circumstance. Thus, there can be growth that moves us from belief to faith and then to knowledge, dispelling doubt. You're right, though, Charles, the easy enumeration of the sequence should not suggest an absence of struggle. But if Moses' people had been intellectually and experientially honest—or had even kept score—they would have been much more trusting as each new challenge arose!

RACHEL: But Charles is correct. Developing faith should never be thought of as a smooth continuum in which is all "Whoopee!" and "Look, no hands!"

PAULINE: I surely agree. In fact, there are times when, for the moment, our faith may seem to have led us into a cul-de-sac. There is no way to go around—we must go through! It must have been so at the edge of the Red Sea! The people railed at Moses for taking them away from Egypt. Listen to these words from Exodus: "Is not this the word that we did tell thee in Egypt, saying, Let us alone, that we may serve the Egyptians? For it had been better for us to serve the Egyptians, than that we should die in the wilderness." (Exodus 14:12.)

Jeffrey and I then pondered these sobering verses in Exodus in preparation for our discussion: "And Moses said unto the people, Fear ye not, stand still, and see the salvation of the Lord, which he will shew to you to day: for the Egyptians whom ye have seen to day, ye shall see them again no more for ever. The Lord shall fight for you, and ye shall hold your peace." (Exodus 14:13, 14.)

NOEL: "Stand still" and "hold your peace"—marvelous imagery, Pauline, and how soberingly instructive. Thank you.

Unlike those ancient Israelites, once we are settled in our minds, surely we need not overreact to each new crisis or criticism or each new fiery dart of doubt any more than we who are scientists need to recheck the chemical composition of water to be sure, one more time, that it consists of two parts hydrogen—not three—and one part oxygen.

WINSTON: That is your earlier point, isn't it? We should not demand of God "perpetual renewal of absolute truth." Past validating experience should, if we're intellectually honest, actually count for something!

JEFFREY: You put it well, Winston. In a sense, God's

past contributions to our supply of spiritual knowledge do give Him an equity position in believers, don't they?

NOEL: But His claim on us as a result of past investments and blessings is unacknowledged or brushed aside by most mortals, isn't it?

RACHEL: A Relief Society sister said the other day that without God's past blessings to her, she'd have little reason to hope for further blessings now. But she goes on enduring well, because, as Jeffrey reminded us, she has proven God in "days that are past."

CHARLES: Without such faith as hers, however, so many people have concluded that life is pointless and hopeless. Even after all that some of them have accomplished or become, they sometimes forlornly say of their existence, "Is this all there is? Am I, as an individual entity, to be expunged, to be consumed into nothingness?" Extinction!

NOEL: Joseph Smith once spoke of a vision he had of the dead and their actual resurrection and of the comfort this vision gave, since, to him, the thought of annihilation was much more painful than death. Joseph went on to express his gratitude that God had revealed His Son from the heavens and also given the doctrine of the resurrection.[5] Alma at first even desired his actual extinction—body and soul! But, happily, he remembered the words of his father about an atoning Jesus. Then came his great soul cry: "Now, as my mind caught hold upon this thought, I cried within my heart: O Jesus, thou son of God, have mercy on me." (Alma 36:15-18.)

PAULINE: And what a "soul cry" that was: "O Jesus,

thou Son of God"! How precious and actuating are the words of Alma's father. I must have passed over those lines without pondering them.

NOEL: Pauline, apparently you've noticed, too, how the Lord seems to slip new verses into the scriptures since we last read them.

WINSTON: So, you're saying, Noel, that, once the footings of faith are in place, there is a process of re-inforcing accumulation and accretion? As I think about it, it's not likely, for instance, that marvelous Mother Teresa in India would suddenly denounce the poor, among whom she has spent so much of her life, or lose interest in sick children, so many of whom she has saved.

RACHEL: Indeed not. But we mustn't forget the fundamental focus of our faith. We would scarcely have sufficient confidence to experiment, as Alma urged, on Jesus' word if we did not at least desire to believe in Jesus.

CHARLES: Yet new tests do come along, don't they? The adversary can carry out what C. S. Lewis called "a blitz" on our belief in certain principles. We are far too much at the mercy of our moods—which shift—even when the massive and impressive divine data hold still. At least I confess to having this vulnerability at times.

NOEL: Charles, for all of us, mood and mind are inter-active. Some moods put a momentary, dark cloud cover over us—not because any of the basic spiritual data have changed, however. Rather, just as you're saying, because our moods can cause us to mistake today's cloud cover for general darkness.

CHARLES: Or to mistake the startling sound of a single rifle shot for the menacing sound of an approaching army, causing doubt without data and panic without cause. Some individuals have so much fear of being taken in that they remain forever outside!

WINSTON: Hmmm. Yet, a mind furnished with fixed faith, that is honest with regard to past experimentation with gospel principles, should, presumably, apply itself quickly and gladly to new tests and circumstances. It isn't all that easy, though, is it?

RACHEL: No, it isn't, especially if we merely skim over the surface of the gospel.

NOEL: How true. We may, for a while, feel secure and even satisfied by merely being able to describe with precision the anatomy of faith, its words and rituals, its sounds and shadows, instead of becoming experienced in the substance of faith. But such superficiality cannot sustain us for long.

There is no other way. We must deepen our faith until it becomes the real thing. Otherwise, when the heat of the day comes, if we are not, to use Peter and Paul's words, "grounded," "rooted," "established," and "settled," we will wither under the scorching summer of circumstances. (Matthew 13:6; Ephesians 3:17; Colossians 1:23; 1 Peter 5:10; Alma 32:38.)

CHARLES: Are you saying, Noel, that untried faith may not be real faith at all?

NOEL: I'm not fully sure, but probably. Has not the Lord even told us that He will try the faith and the patience of His people? Why then are we surprised when our faith is tried? (Mosiah 23:21.) The Lord may actually be offering us new data, new knowledge, new and needed reinforcement—but disguised as a trial.

WINSTON: But it doesn't come cost free, does it? Besides, it seems to me that trying our patience surely involves our trust in God. Do we trust Him adequately? Waiting and enduring thus become so vital.

NOEL: A telling point! For instance, the children of Israel and even some of their leaders grew impatient when Moses delayed coming down from Sinai. (Exodus 32:1.) It was lack of faith in the Lord, combined with impatience, that produced the golden calf!

JEFFREY: Our faith is not tried, however, because God is uncertain about the outcome, given His foreknowledge and omniscience. Rather, so that, as we pass through these particularized experiences, our thoughts, attitudes, and behavior—at that time and with regard to a particular dimension of faith—will be incontestably inscribed in the Book of Life. (Revelation 20:12.) No valid protests can be lodged later.

NOEL: Furthermore, it seems to me that our faith is almost always tried not so much in regard to general propositions but with regard to particular circumstances—in this matter or in "that thing." Isn't it so?

It is while we are in the midst of these that we sometimes feel perplexed, frustrated, angry, or even forsaken.

RACHEL: Yes! We see through a glass only darkly, but we naturally desire to see the "end" from the "beginning." (1 Corinthians 13:12.) We are experiencing, instead, at the moment, the mortal middle.

CHARLES: The murky middle!

PAULINE: Such murky and vexing circumstances do require a special and specific faith in a God whose purposes are loving. And we can surely come to know "that thing" as Rachel said, namely, that God loves us perfectly and personally!

Nephi stated it so very well: "I know that [God] loveth his children; nevertheless, I do not know the meaning of all things." (1 Nephi 11:17.)

WINSTON: Alas, such operational faith, the day-in and day-out steadiness, is anything but easy to acquire and retain. I suppose this should not be surprising, since acquiring such faith is both a central purpose and a crowning achievement in one's life. After all, we are to walk by faith, and to "overcome by faith." (D&C 76:53.)

JEFFREY: Exactly! I was impressed, as Pauline and I prepared for tonight, that there must be both definite and adequate time provided for the good seed of the gospel to work. Meanwhile, we are not to grow impatient and cast out the good seed by our bad moods or our unbelief. (Alma 32:28.) We are to nourish it patiently and to give it time to grow and sprout.

NOEL: And, Jeffrey, not be forever pulling up the tiny tree of testimony to see how the roots are doing!

WINSTON: Hmmm. Faith is not faith like Jonah's gourd, is it? It does not spring up, full blown, overnight! (Jonah 4:6.)

RACHEL: Remember those terrestrial souls who are honorable individuals but are "not valiant in the testimony of Jesus"? (D&C 76:79.) It is not that fair-weather faith but sustained and focused faith that we are discussing tonight.

CHARLES: However, unless the seed is growing, it seems so easy for one's faith to slide back to belief. And for this belief to slide back into unbelief, is it not?

Especially upon encountering a new matter or a new "thing." Did not some believers, even upon seeing the resurrected Jesus, still wonder?

JEFFREY: Yes. Give me a moment . . . Here, please listen to these verses from Luke and Mark in support of what Charles just said: "And [they] returned from the sepulchre, and told all these things unto the eleven, and to all the rest. It was Mary Magdalene, and Joanna, and Mary the mother of James, and other women that were with them, which told these things unto the apostles. And their words seemed to them as idle tales, and they believed them not." (Luke 24:9-11.)

"Now when Jesus was risen early the first day of the week, he appeared first to Mary Magdalene, out of whom he had cast seven devils. And she went and told them that had been with him, as they mourned and wept. And they, when they had heard that he was alive, and had been seen of her, believed not." (Mark 16:9-11.)

NOEL: Excellent illustrations, Jeffrey, showing how faith is adventure into what is a comparatively unknown realm for us but a realm perfectly known to God, of course.

It is precisely at this point we encounter one of the most marvelous yet paradoxical truths of the gospel! The more we venture by keeping the commandments, the more God can teach us. The more we venture by obeying Him, the more our faith is turned into knowledge.

In the 6th Lecture on Faith it is said of the members of the Church "that unless they have an actual knowledge that the course they are pursuing is according to the will of God they will grow weary in their minds, and faint."[6] A fascinating insight.

RACHEL: Noel's point gives me a chance to report something our eldest daughter and I were discussing the other day. Unfortunately, some of her college chums are drifting from gospel standards by doing the wrong kind of experimenting. She found the courage to say to them, the less we behave, the more dark the mind; the less we know, the less our faith; the less our belief, the more we slide into unbelief. I was proud of her.

WINSTON: But Rachel, isn't what you and Noel are saying somewhat like the American governor who once said of his troubled state prison that the prison could be upgraded only when they got a better quality of prisoners!

NOEL: Not really, Winston. Listen to how closely John and Alma support Jesus and each other with regard to doing and knowing. Jesus said, "If any man will do his will, he shall know of the doctrine, whether it be of God, or whether I speak of myself." (John 7:17.)

Alma said, "And now, behold, because ye have tried the experiment, and planted the seed, and it swelleth and sprouteth, and beginneth to grow, ye must needs know that the seed is good. And now, behold, is your knowledge perfect? Yea, your knowledge is perfect in that thing, and your faith is dormant; and this because ye know, for ye know that the word hath swelled your souls, and ye also know that it hath sprouted up, that your understanding doth begin to be enlightened, and your mind doth begin to expand." (Alma 32:33-34.)

Thus, behaving and knowing do feed upon each other, resulting in what Paul called "the evidence of things not seen." (Hebrews 11:1.) Interestingly enough,

Orson Pratt wrote, "When God reveals a truth, . . . it is always accompanied by sufficient evidence."[7]

JEFFREY: By the way, the Prophet Joseph was equally declarative regarding how virtue and verity are companions in the journey of life. He said, "Be virtuous and pure; be men of integrity and truth; keep the commandments of God; and then you will be able more perfectly to understand the difference between right and wrong—between the things of God and the things of men; and your path will be like that of the just, which shineth brighter and brighter unto the perfect day."[8]

CHARLES: So, alas, Jeffrey, are misbehavior and doubt companions; they produce reciprocity, too!

But what I want to say is this: I'm impressed that the danger of holding back and of hesitancy is so real. It is the very trap into which some of us fall!

NOEL: Quite so, for there are those who are "slow of heart to believe." (Luke 24:25.) Moroni advised us that we receive no witness until *after—not before*—the trial of our faith. (Ether 12:6.)

CHARLES: Not a very comforting declaration, that one.

NOEL: But it fits with all else said tonight regarding how faith can become knowledge. Jesus is not asking us to be naive or superficial. Instead, we are to act in a manner consistent with our past spiritual experiences. Having trusted in God successfully before, we can now trust Him yet again.

WINSTON: Forgive my periodic references to things governmental, but such settled trust and faith was evident in Shadrach, Meshach, and Abed-nego. The King marveled, when they emerged from the fiery furnace, that they displayed no hurt, no hair singed, nor even the smell of fire. (Daniel 3:24-27.) Apparently there were no first-amendment freedoms to protect those believers then.

RACHEL: But the Lord protected them because they trusted Him so, as expressed in these verses: "If it be so, our God whom we serve is able to deliver us from the burning fiery furnace, and he will deliver us out of thine hand, O king. But if not, be it known unto thee, O king, that we will not serve thy gods, nor worship the golden image which thou hast set up." (Daniel 3:17-18.)

WINSTON: Those declarative words "but if not" are so faith filled.

PAULINE: I wish we knew more about the three young women who were equally valiant.

WINSTON: Which three women, Pauline?

PAULINE: The three virgin daughters of Onitah, a descendent of Ham, who were sacrificed because they would not worship gods of wood or stone. It's all in the first chapter of Abraham. (Abraham 1:11.)

WINSTON: I'd never really noticed that verse, Pauline. I join you in wishing we knew more! Yet, for me, though I am making progress, it is still tough going. It's not difficult believing in what happened to these three men. I do! But it's tough to face my own challenges, to survive amid my little fiery furnaces. Sorry, but I need and miss my wife so much. Surely God knew how much our family needs her!

NOEL: Perhaps the key for all of us, Winston, whatever our fiery trial, includes what Peter said: not to be surprised. (1 Peter 4:12.) Then, just as did those six gallant women and men, to have the Lord at our side! But you have come much farther along the path than you may realize, Winston.

WINSTON: I need and want that Divine support so much . . .

CHARLES: I concur with Noel about how far you've come, Winston. It has helped me to try harder.

Wordsworth was not far off. He described such an intact individual as you are becoming as "One in whom persuasion and belief / Had ripened into faith, and faith become / A passionate intuition."[9]

RACHEL: Thank you, Charles, for saying what I, too, see happening to Winston. Now, in near conclusion, may Noel and I review a few final scriptures and episodes? Noel, shall I start? Out of these comments Noel and I will give in tandem, we can perhaps squeeze some concluding generalizations.

In that episode on Galilee when Jesus walked on the water, remember that Peter first asked Jesus to beckon him to come? Jesus did. Then Peter walked on water, however briefly. He is the only mortal to have done so, as far as we know. However, Peter did it not for display, but in order "to go to Jesus." (Matthew 14:29.)

NOEL: It was only when he saw the "wind boisterous" that he became afraid and began to sink. Even though Peter no longer walked on water, he had not lost his faith in Jesus' power to save Him. He cried out to Jesus, "Save me," fearing he would drown. Jesus then extended His hand to Peter, both catching him and re-proving him because Peter had doubted. (Matthew 14:30-31.)

CHARLES: How loving yet tutoring! Perhaps it was Peter's failure to keep his eye fixed on Jesus? Like the not fully committed plowman? Instead of looking straight ahead at Jesus, Peter looked around, com-puted the odds, and was terrified. As any of us would be! How does one ignore wind-whipped whitecaps?

RACHEL: But if we are willing to proceed with our eye upon Jesus Christ instead of upon all that might go wrong, or upon the waves pounding and swirling about us, if we "go to Jesus" directly, knowing that He can save us, we will not be forsaken either. Even if we seem to be sinking, we are still to reach out to Him.

PAULINE: Oh, the fierce interplay of faith and cir-cumstance! Remember another occasion when the dis-ciples were on a tempestuous Galilee sea? The boat was filling with water. Fearful of the wind and of pos-sible loss of life, they awakened a slumbering Jesus only to be reproved because they had no faith. (Mark 4:37-40.)

NOEL: Thanks, Pauline, for that companion scripture. Once again, however, it was the terrifying circum-stances around them that called their faith into ques-tion.

James said it well, didn't he? If we doubt, we be-come like those very waves, tossed by the wind! (James 1:6.)

CHARLES: There are always uncertain souls, how-ever, milling about in Joel's "valley of decision." (Joel 3:14.) Sometimes I feel an unwanted identity with them.

I brought along one of my favorite C. S. Lewis quotations, by the way.

*(Knowing smiles cross every face because of Charles's penchant for Lewis.)*

CHARLES: It describes the two-way traffic, going toward and away from the Lord: "There are people (a great many of them) who are slowly ceasing to be Christians but who still call themselves by that name: some of them are clergymen. There are other people who are slowly becoming Christians though they do not yet call themselves so.

"There are people who do not accept the full Christian doctrine about Christ but who are so strongly attracted by Him that they are His in a much deeper sense than they themselves understand. There are people in other religions who are being led by God's secret influence to concentrate on those parts of their religion which are in agreement with Christianity, and who thus belong to Christ without knowing it. . . . And always, of course, there are a great many people who are just confused in mind and have a lot of inconsistent beliefs all jumbled up together. Consequently, it is not much use trying to make judgements about Christians and non-Christians in the mass."[10]

NOEL: Charles has provided the summation again. The evening has been well spent, but the clock is running. We'll plan to talk more about faith next time. •

CHARLES: May we add to our growing agendum for future discussion not only prayer but the nature of spiritual knowledge? I need help in relating spiritual knowledge to secular knowledge.

PAULINE: Another postscript request, Noel. Could we take a moment sometime to talk of the Resurrected

Christ and what we know of His work after His resurrection?

NOEL: Perhaps in a later discussion. It is speculation, however, as to the entirety of what the resurrected Jesus did. After His appearance to His disciples in the Holy Land, He visited with some of His disciples in the Americas. (3 Nephi 11.) He indicated at the time that He had still other sheep He was to visit. (3 Nephi 16:1-3.)

PAULINE: I mean even beyond. The eighty-eighth section of the Doctrine and Covenants contains a parable that is so intriguing. It speaks of other kingdoms moving in their majesty, being inhabited, and visited. In fact, to try to persuade or intrigue you, Noel, I brought along some poetry. Alice Meynell wrote so beautifully of "Christ in the Universe," of His "earth-visiting feet" on "our wayside planet." Her lines are so precious and evocative: "May His devices with the heavens be guessed;/ His pilgrimage to thread the Milky Way,/ Or His bestowals there, be manifest./ But, in the eternities,/ Doubtless we shall compare together, hear/ A million alien Gospels, in what guise/ He trod the Pleiades, the Lyre, the Bear."

NOEL: But poetry is not theology . . .

*(It is clearly a moment that matters very much to Pauline. Noel suddenly feels ashamed for being so insensitive.)*

RACHEL: But it can be, Noel! We read of Christ . . . just a moment . . . here it is: "That by him, and through him, and of him, the worlds are and were created, and the inhabitants thereof are begotten sons and daughters unto God." (D&C 76:24.)

NOEL: Thank you very much, Pauline, for those lines of Meynell's that I, at least, have not heard before! While we must leave to further revelation the matter of any possible triumphal tour by Jesus after the resurrection, it is intriguing indeed to ponder. We can add it to our list of future topics, but what little can be safely said may have already been said in our exchange just now.

Charles, was it not Lewis who said that for the Christian, "the cross comes before the crown, and tomorrow is a Monday morning"?

# Second Conversation:
# The Justice of God

"Thus came the voice of the Lord unto me,
saying: All who have died without a knowledge
of this gospel, who would have received it if
they had been permitted to tarry, shall be heirs
of the celestial kingdom of God; also all that
shall die henceforth without a knowledge of it,
who would have received it with all their hearts,
shall be heirs of that kingdom; for I, the Lord,
will judge all men according to their works,
according to the desire of their hearts."
(D&C 137:7-9.)

**The setting:** *Noel, Winston, and Charles, in lieu of lunch,
are walking slowly through a park. Their stroll is punctuated
by periodic pauses as they circle for ease of discussion and also
because of the intensity of the discussion. Their conversation
centers upon the justice of God and the unresponsiveness of
mankind to His message.*

CHARLES: Noel, one of the things that presses in upon me and, in a sense, even discourages me, at least at times, is the tremendous mass of humanity who live out their days on this planet never even having heard of Jesus Christ, let alone receiving the fulness of His gospel . . .

NOEL: With your keen sensitivity to the needs of others, Charles, that's a natural and even commendable concern. Let me try to respond. According to the revelation given to Joseph Smith about his deceased brother Alvin, all who would have received the gospel with fulness of heart and intent while upon this earth, who received it later beyond the veil, will receive all of the same blessings and rewards. (D&C 137: 7-9.)

CHARLES: I know, I know. That is part of the eventual justice of God. It's not that which worries me so much. Rather, it's the slender portion of humanity for whom the gospel plan operates fully in this life. It seems such a small number.

NOEL: The eventual outcome is consistent, however, with Jesus' declaration that, ultimately, "strait is the gate, and narrow is the way, which leadeth unto life, and few there be that find it." (Matthew 7:14.) Besides, meanwhile, the chance to choose God in the second estate does not end with death; it continues into the spirit world until the final judgment and resurrection. There will be a chance for all.

CHARLES: I realize that, too, but when the lamentable paucity of those who are blessed with the fulness of the gospel during their earthly probation is joined with the exclusive claims of the Church, I become troubled.

WINSTON: I can't forget, Charles, what we discussed in earlier conversations about God's commitment to the moral agency of man. His commitment carries real and constant consequences with it.

Nevertheless, I have pondered this same enormous question many times. In my own mind, I have found it helpful to assume there may be "givens" within which even God Himself works, agency being a major one. Another, perhaps, is the personality and character of each of us, God's spirit children. Whatever, if anything, we may have brought with us by way of individual proclivities into our spirit birth long ago may constitute constraints within which even God works, though this is speculation. We must have brought luggage with us, much more recently, from our first estate into this second estate.

In any event, if you put this factor with God's deep and enormous commitment to our agency, the outcome inevitably is one that is very uneven and in which there must be patience and long-suffering as a loving Father works out His plan of salvation. No wonder the bulk of the work must be done, as Noel said, beyond the veil—at least numerically speaking—before a final judgment.

Odd, isn't it, how so many mortals denounce or deny God because He will not denounce our moral agency? Yet most human misery occurs because we mortals misuse and abuse our agency. But it's God who gets scolded or denied because of such suffering, when, in fact, as a long-suffering Father, He steadfastly supports His plan of salvation in which our agency is key.

CHARLES: I find that especially helpful, Winston. Even so, you can see why it causes me concern, can't you?

WINSTON: Yes. But God's love of his children and of liberty is so very, very deep!

NOEL: I understand your concerns too, Charles. Walking as we must by faith, we simply do not have all the revelation or information we desire, especially concerning our dim beginnings. We still see through a glass darkly. We are left, therefore, with pondering over matters such as you have just mentioned.

Perhaps the exclusivity matter also needs to be put into yet another perspective. Given the perfect love, mercy, and justice of God, neither the seeming exclusivity of Jesus' declaration about the strait and narrow way nor His statement about His latter-day Church should concern us overmuch. (See D&C 1:30.) Such does not suggest exclusivity as to human decency or goodness, nor does it suggest any exclusivity as to the bestowal of God's love. The basic human decency of so many people on this planet, their love of goodness and of God, their devotion even to Jesus Christ—many of them at least—is so clear. This is because the Light of Christ, or conscience, lights every soul to some degree. (John 1:9; Moroni 7:16, 18-19.) Furthermore, each soul is credited by God with all good works he has done in this life. And every soul, before the judgment, has a full chance to receive the gospel and is rewarded just as if he had received the gospel in mortality. Our concerns should be eased.

CHARLES: That is helpful, too.

WINSTON: Perhaps, Charles, you'll need to hold this one in abeyance.

CHARLES: I'm already holding too many things in abeyance, Winston. I need to achieve some resolution.

NOEL: Charles, the issue is large. Given our moral agency and whatever proclivities we brought with us, this life will not produce proximate justice or evenness of opportunity, in the short term, for people to hear the gospel. But if, prior to the judgment, as is certainly the case, all will have an *equal* opportunity and an *equal* chance to hear the gospel and to accept or reject it, such would, of course, erase or ease any ultimate concern.

Besides, biblical and other scriptural history makes it clear that God has worked before through chosen people—imperfect as they were—to do His work. This pattern is merely operating again in our time.

WINSTON: But being chosen is a call to work, not a designation of status, isn't it?

CHARLES: I suppose so. What do you suppose it is that bothers me about exclusivity?

NOEL: Please forgive me, Charles, but could it be false pride?

CHARLES: What do you mean?

NOEL: I mean you may be anxious because you have been put on the spot as one chosen of God for special benefits and blessings that do not now come to 99 percent of the human family, as you've already pointed out. If so, as Winston noted, you've merely been designated to do God's work, which is real and demanding. Furthermore, Charles, hasn't a just Lord said that His blessings come by obedience to specific laws? (D&C 130:20-21.) He does not distribute His blessings capriciously in this second estate, nor did He in the first.

WINSTON: I can never read the thirteenth chapter of Alma—let me find it in my pocket-sized scriptures— and feel other than sobered and humbled, especially when I read this verse: "This is the manner after which they were ordained—being called and prepared from the foundation of the world according to the fore-knowledge of God, on account of their exceeding faith and good works; in the first place being left to choose good or evil; therefore they having chosen good, and exercising exceedingly great faith, are called with a holy calling, yea, with the holy calling which was pre-pared with, and according to, a preparatory redemp-tion for such." (Alma 13:3.)

NOEL: Perhaps, along with the rest of us, Charles, you feel understandably inadequate and unworthy. But perhaps even more deeply for you at least now, there is also some inner anxiety about the nature of a God who would be presiding over such a plan. I hope what has been said has been helpful.

CHARLES: Your words have found their mark, Noel. Thanks for being lovingly candid. The disdain of others concerning the exclusivity of Jesus Christ, His gospel, and His Church being the "one way" does trouble me.

At bottom, what may have been bothering me, just as Noel suggested, is not a concern over God's mercy or redemptiveness but, in a sense, feeling "put on the spot" by Him. Being put up against . . . not just the scorn of people, which in some ways would be easier to bear, but being put up against their incredulity! How a small group of people—then or now—could so regard themselves as being so special or chosen! Espe-cially in today's seemingly sophisticated world.

NOEL: But one can know, by the Spirit, that Jesus' "one way" is the only way. Fortified by such knowl-edge, one can endure taunts or disdain. Besides, each soul, sooner or later, is free to choose whether or not to accept Jesus and to walk the strait and narrow path.

But he or she is not free to re-define the parameters of that path. The doctrines, said Jesus, are not His, but the Father's. (John 7:17.) These doctrines are not ours to revise either.

WINSTON: And aren't we glad? Another possibly helpful point, Charles, is that the redemptiveness of God is spread out over such an expanse of time and space, extending into eternity. As a loving God, He never forsakes His children or quits trying to redeem them. We dare not lecture Him regarding the plight of His children.

CHARLES: And you are saying, Noel, that I had better not overreact to any particular band of time on that long spectrum? Simply because so little seems to be getting accomplished at the moment?

NOEL: Yes. And we are even counseled to be patient amid criticism. Some criticism may be put down at once, but the Lord's promise was and is that voices lifted against His cause "shall be confounded" but "in mine own due time." (D&C 71:10.)

CHARLES: Sometimes I wish He'd hurry!

NOEL: God has been at His work for such a very long time! In fact, His course is one eternal round. (Alma 37:12; D&C 3:2.) And He has also said certain things must be done in His own due time. (D&C 24:16; 35:25.)

WINSTON: Back to the matter of whatever luggage we brought with us into our birth long ago as God's spirit children. If, as mentioned earlier, along with identity, there was any individual proclivity, this would make God's deep commitment to agency and His patience and longsuffering not only so commendable but also even more understandable, wouldn't it?

CHARLES: It surely would! This has been so helpful. I appreciate your patience with me on this matter, because it's so central.

WINSTON: Indeed it is. And it is worthy of any time and prayerful pondering an individual can give it. Noel, you're the scientist. I wish we could express all this in equation form. We could take X, an unknown quantity that constitutes each individual entity, plus moral agency plus time to get a spiritual sum, an outcome that to us, while the equation was in process, would seem uneven and uncertain, producing some of the concerns Charles has mentioned.

NOEL: *(Chuckling.)* I'm afraid no such equation is possible. But with all the data cranked in, and if examined longitudinally, the outcome would underscore the perfect love, justice, and mercy of God! Your remarks remind me of some reassuring words in Jeremiah: "I the Lord search the heart, I try the reins, even to give every man according to his ways, and according to the fruit of his doings." (Jeremiah 17:10.) How God honors our agency, thus balancing His love, justice, and mercy against the diversity and enormity of the size of the human family! Also thus balancing God's omniscience and man's moral agency.

CHARLES: There are some very stubborn sheep in His fold to whom God happily gives the gift of time as well as agency. Perhaps most of our chafing occurs because of false pride and because of the imperfect operation of the Lord's Church and the imperfect implementation of the gospel's perfect principles.

NOEL: Well said. There is so much we do not yet know for which we must simply trust Him, as our circle of friends concluded the other night. Just as we trusted

God before for what we have since come to know, we
should also trust Him for what we do not know. Once
God's perfected attributes of mercy, knowledge, love,
and patience are truly accepted by us, then we will accept that these qualities will operate throughout the
length and breadth and depth of His plan, producing
justice, mercy, and redemption by salvation and exal-
tation. Exclusivity couldn't be a sustained worry if we
understood the basic truths about the nature of God
and how He works within an eternal perspective.

CHARLES: But we would still feel the pressure from
others meanwhile, wouldn't we?

NOEL: We would and do! Again, however, Jesus certainly didn't worry over the exclusivity of His declaration. In fact, He went against the grain of His time in a
most heroic and courageous manner, never down-
playing His mission or His identity as the Redeemer
and the Messiah. Jesus surely did not shrink from declaring and acknowledging His true identity. (See
John 5:19; 7:16; 8:18; 13:13, 14.) Yet timing mattered
then, too. Listen: "Then charged he his disciples that
they should tell no man that he was Jesus the Christ."
(Matthew 16:20.)

WINSTON: Now that I think of it, surely Jesus knew, at
the moment He was performing His ministry in the
Holy Land, that little was being done, then, among the
millions of people then living in what we know today
as China.

Trusting in the timing of God is, therefore, part of
our particularized faith in Him! He's surely not trying
to keep anyone out of His kingdom who truly wishes
to be there, whether on one side of the veil or the
other.

NOEL: In fact, the Lord said to Oliver Cowdery not to "suppose that he can say enough in my cause." (D&C 24:10.) And the Twelve were told to labor "morning by morning" and "day after day." They were also told that they should "let not the inhabitants of the earth slumber, because of [their] speech." (D&C 112:5.)

CHARLES: Meanwhile, quite clearly, we are bound to be taunted by criticisms of exclusivity. Our only choice, therefore, appears to be to respond by Christian living and loving, as did Jesus, let others say what they will, I suppose.

NOEL: Yes, it matters very little what others think of us, but it matters very much what we think of Christ. (Matthew 7:21-23.) It matters little who others say we are but very much Who we say Christ is and whether or not we're truly trying to live His teachings. If the adversary wished to create discomfort and doubt—

CHARLES: And surely he does!

NOEL: —It would be quite natural for him to attack believers at some basic points.

CHARLES: An excellent observation, Noel. It fits beautifully with what one of you said recently about the adversary seeking the "crown jewels."

NOEL: He's not likely, is he, to focus his attack on the adequacy of the filing system in the ward meetinghouse library or the fairness of the refereeing in the Church's athletic program?

CHARLES: Though he might use, could he not, someone's being offended over refereeing as a means of getting them to be inactive?

NOEL: Indeed he could and perhaps he occasionally

does. But if he wants to have a general unsettling of the people or create an uproar, he would probably try to do this around central issues, hoping to affect large numbers of members who are not sufficiently grounded, rooted, established, and settled.

CHARLES: One of the ironies that comes to mind as we talk about how the vast expanse of time in which God is doing His work overlaps from the first estate into the second estate is this: Those who wish to explain the human condition in nonspiritual terms see vast expanses of time as necessary to man's evolving development. Yet some such individuals are apparently not willing to give God the same amount of time in which to work out His purposes.

WINSTON: As usual, Charles, you have a great capacity for summation. I find, too, that some who unhesitatingly assert that there is legitimate authority in the realms of art, music, and literature ironically accept no authority whatsoever as to morality.

NOEL: So true, Winston! Moreover, the possibility of moral absolutes worries some of them so much that they attack the mere suggestion! The very taunts made of Jesus at critical points, "If thou be the son of God . . . " and so on, have their equivalents that are hurled against the Church institutionally and against its members for proclaiming gospel truths—on a different scale, of course, but just as real and just as pointed, sometimes devastating the unprepared. But Jesus passed through these, and on our scale so must we. (Matthew 27: 40, 42; John 16:33.)

CHARLES: I had not thought of it all in just that way. We have to be especially careful, then, to reflect Christian behavior, lest those taunts find their mark.

NOEL: Wasn't it Peter or Paul who said that if any speak derogatively of believing Christians, let what they say be unjustified? (Matthew 5:11; Titus 2:7-8; 1 Peter 2:12.) In fact, it seems to me that the more the adversary can get us to react to each other's imperfections, the more he can deflect us from perfect principles.

CHARLES: You mean get us to behave like quarreling children—"You did!" "I did not!"—that sort of thing?

NOEL: Precisely! Focusing on the imperfections in Church members as reflected in history. Preoccupation with the past can keep us from facing and shaping the future or from using the holy present.

WINSTON: It's an old trick—impugn the messenger and impugn the message! Is this not Jesus, the carpenter's son? (Matthew 13:55.) On this very point it seems likely, especially as the adversary sees he's running out of time, that he will redouble his assaults. Any individual imperfections in Church members will be trumpeted in his effort to hurt God's work. Satan has no mercy, so we cannot count on any empathy from that quarter!

CHARLES: But Winston, Judas's betrayal of the Savior did not detract from the validity or beauty of the Savior's Sermon on the Mount.

WINSTON: But Judas's betrayal must have hurt the work some then, and failures on our part today will hurt the work, though in the long run the work will prevail.

NOEL: True. Our individual weaknesses will be regarded by some critics as institutional weaknesses. But, as Paul wrote, the Church is for the perfecting of the Saints (Ephesians 4:12.) and, since the Church is filled with imperfect individuals, one should not expect an ecclesiastical Eden!

CHARLES: You're saying, Noel, that when perfect principles are in the minds and hands of imperfect people, their reach will exceed their grasp and their agency will exceed their perceptivity?

NOEL: I wish I had said that, Charles! Excellently put!

WINSTON: Well, this has not been a conversation on the road to Emmaus (Luke 24:13-15), but similar purposes have been served. And on a path in a park filled with trees whose leaves form a symphony of autumn colors.

CHARLES: *Symphony* is just the right word, Winston, for the inner harmony this precious conversation has produced in me. My friends, thanks to both of you.

# Third Conversation: Eternal Assurances

"We talk of Christ, we rejoice in Christ,
we preach of Christ, we prophesy of Christ, and
we write . . . that our children may know to
what source they may look."
(2 Nephi 25:26.)

*The setting:* *In a private dining alcove Noel and Charles are engaged in a lengthy luncheon discussion. Once again the focus is on the need for faith in the reality of God the Father and the Lord Jesus Christ as well as the reality of the resurrection. The particular challenge of believing amid so much unbelief is also discussed.*

————————

CHARLES: I'm bothered by the academic environment I'm in, Noel, by its incessant and pervasive atmosphere not just of skepticism but of deep disbelief,

which makes it such tough going. Whole books are
written announcing God's death, articulate books
such as Michael Harrington's *The Politics at God's Funeral*, that discuss what the eternal silences of the
infinite mean to modern man. So many of my colleagues, on this and other campuses, say, in effect, to
quote an able, articulate skeptic, that man is confronted with "godless geometric space."[1]

NOEL:  But Charles, you're merely making the case for
the need of a grand restoration of the truths affirming
the existence of a loving, succeeding personal God, of
a real and resurrected Savior, of the reality of the resurrection for all mortals. These are the very fundamentals of faith!

CHARLES:  But very few people nowadays have a New
Testament view of the world or really believe in a lit-
eral resurrection. More and more individuals question
the existence of a historical Jesus.

NOEL:  Again, Charles, what more resounding response could God give to such a need than the First
Vision? Or the appearance, in our time, of yet other
resurrected beings, real individuals from biblical
times? It shouldn't surprise us that such spiritual
events are mocked and resented, though. You'll recall
how the chief priests wanted to murder the restored
Lazarus, who was Exhibit A of Jesus' divinity. (John
12:2-11.) A restored Lazarus threatened some then just
as a restored Church threatens some now!

CHARLES:  A fair rebuttal indeed! But you see what I'm
up against.

NOEL:  You're up against just what Nephi and others
foresaw about the need for additional affirming scrip-

ture to establish the truth of the Bible. Let me read from Nephi: "After [the Bible] had come forth unto them I beheld other books, which came forth by the power of the Lamb, from the Gentiles unto them, unto the convincing of the Gentiles and the remnant of the seed of my brethren, and also the Jews who were scattered upon all the face of the earth, that the records of the prophets and of the twelve apostles of the Lamb are true. And the angel spake unto me, saying: These last records, which thou hast seen among the Gentiles, shall establish the truth of the first, which are of the twelve apostles of the Lamb, and shall make known the plain and precious things which have been taken away from them; and shall make known to all kindreds, tongues, and people, that the Lamb of God is the Son of the Eternal Father, and the Savior of the world; and that all men must come unto him, or they cannot be saved." (1 Nephi 13:39, 40.)

CHARLES: "Other books," "convincing," "plain and precious things," and testifying of our Savior. Noel, the significance of those verses has never really penetrated my mind before. What is "out there" is not "godless geometric space" but a universe being managed by an omnicompetent, loving Father-God. There are such enormous implications flowing from the central revelation that Jesus is the Christ . . . but . . .

NOEL: Since Jesus is the chief cornerstone, He makes it possible for all else that matters to be fitly framed together. Then and only then we see divine design in the large universe and also in our own little universes of experience. But we need real faith to function in both universes.

CHARLES: Frankly, it is precisely the latter that sometimes causes me to falter somewhat. Strangely, I can believe in an overall plan for man much more easily than a specific plan for me! Do you understand?

NOEL: Yes. You're not so unusual. But there is resolving help available. God's revelations, whether in scripture or from living apostles, certainly spare us from having to rely solely upon deduction as we seek to increase our faith. Likewise his revelations spare us from total reliance upon the limitations of induction and of reasoning from part to whole and from particulars to universals. Without revelation, we would merely flail about—or wander within our own conceptual constraints and within the confines of our provincial, personal experiences.

CHARLES: Especially within the confines of our own severely limited experience!

NOEL: I marvel at God's timing in which—at that stage in history, when the crisis of belief was mounting in Christian nations—there came the theophany at Palmyra and all that ensued! What divine anticipation and response to the concerns over a historical Jesus!

CHARLES: But such selective appearances do not help the bulk of mankind.

NOEL: The resurrected Jesus appeared to hundreds in the Holy Land. But you're right, it was selective—to disciples and believers. Since we are to walk by faith, God and Jesus will not overwhelm or intimidate us. Besides, if a people or a person has erroneous expectations, such as about the Messiah, these erroneous expectations will lead to erroneous evaluations just as occurred concerning Jesus of Nazareth. As you know, some expected a conquering Messiah of Bethlehem. (John 7:40-44; Matthew 2:6.) Later the resurrected

Christ appeared to five hundred (1 Corinthians 15:6), but He did not display Himself to the Sanhedrin!

There is yet another cluster of implications flowing from the truths bound up in the plan of salvation, the mother lode of meaning. For instance, by knowing we are sent here to experience mortality, to be clothed in a mortal body, and to undergo the needed proving and tutoring experiences, we would automatically see a baby as something special.

CHARLES: And abortion as heinous! Coincidentally enough, just the other day, I read this commentary in a recent medical journal, which obviously goes against the grain of the gospel, if the words are intended to mean what they say: "Whatever the future holds, it is likely to prove impossible to restore in full the sanctity-of-life view. The philosophical foundations of this view have been knocked asunder. We can no longer base our ethics on the idea that human beings are a special form of creation, made in the image of God, singled out from all other animals, and alone possessing an immortal soul. Our better understanding of our own nature has bridged the gulf that was once thought to lie between ourselves and other species, so why should we believe that the mere fact that a being is a member of the species *Homo sapiens* endows its life with some unique, almost infinite, value?"[2] (*Shakes his head in disapproval.*) The more I ponder the more it all comes down to Jesus and His and our Father's plan of salvation—there is no other way, no other integrated and complete perspective about life.

How the gospel helps us to focus on what really matters by giving us precious perspective, whether about a baby or a family! For instance, as a recently and reluctantly divorced man, there is for me more than passing significance in these words about Lehi: "[He] took nothing with him, save it were his family." (1 Nephi 2:4.) These words have a way of looping through my mind again and again.

NOEL: I'm not surprised. Our press clippings, medals, wardrobes, cars, houses—so many of the transitory things upon which we lavish our time, talents, and treasure—will, in fact, not go with us!

How could we possibly have such perspective, however, without what the revealed gospel gives us through our understanding of the plan of salvation? But confirming personal revelation is still needed to validate the doctrinal revelation reposing in God's Church. Listen to this quotation from President Brigham Young: "I say that the living oracles of God, or the Spirit of revelation must be in each and every individual, to know the plan of salvation and keep in the path that leads them to the presence of God."[3]

CHARLES: Are you saying that perhaps blurred perceptions about the purposes of life account for such diversity in the human responses to the tests of our faith?

NOEL: I am, Charles. When faith-filled Abraham was confronted with the remarkable promises made to him, he had no intellectual or experiential basis to believe. Yet with faith in our Father and our Father's plan, Abraham "staggered not at the promise of God through unbelief." (Romans 4:20.)

CHARLES: "Staggered not" evokes such instructive imagery.

NOEL: It's the natural eye, isn't it, that so quickly sees threatening waves and winds? It is the natural eye that discovers with alarm that the boat is filling with water! (Luke 8:22-24.) It is the natural eye that sees the loss of political position, prestige, or a place in the synagogue. (John 12:42, 43.)

CHARLES: But, as you say, the eye of faith views things otherwise! All true believers can certainly be possessed of adequate personal revelation themselves, and can themselves, therefore, declare Him to be the centerpiece in human history.

NOEL: Can and should! Especially so since Christ is the verification of meaning, hope, and purpose for all mankind. In fact, surrender to Him is clearly the only surrender that is also a victory—an enormous victory. It is also the only global victory whose fruits time and change cannot erode . . . and that may be enjoyed forever!

CHARLES: However, even prophets are still affected by the milieu in which they serve, aren't they? Great and good Moses was affected—and sometimes afflicted—by the people he led.

NOEL: Our small lunch table seems able to accommodate only one set of scriptures. May I read in support of what you just said, Charles? From Numbers: "Moses said unto the Lord, Wherefore hast thou afflicted thy servant? and wherefore have I not found favour in thy sight, that thou layest the burden of all this people upon me? . . . I am not able to bear all this people alone, because it is too heavy for me. . . . And Moses said, . . . Would God that all the Lord's people were prophets, and that the Lord would put his spirit upon them!" (Numbers 11:11, 14, 29.) Moses also said, "Behold, they will not believe me, nor hearken unto my voice: for they will say, The Lord hath not appeared unto thee." (Exodus 4:1.) But even in the midst of his concerns, Moses persisted, and "the people believed: and when they heard that the Lord had visited the children of Israel, and that he had looked upon their affliction, then they bowed their heads and worshipped." (Exodus 4:31.)

CHARLES: Yet even the past spiritual experiences of a whole people seem to need reinforcing. Unless their faith is kept active and vibrantly alive, they will not have the faith required in the matter of the moment, the challenge of the day. May I borrow your scriptures, Noel? Mine are at home in my study, where I try to overcome the loneliness of a large house.

Nephi had, on a smaller scale, the same challenge as Moses. Here it is. Among Lehi's entourage were the reluctant and critical: "My brethren did complain against me, and were desirous that they might not labor, for they did not believe that I could build a ship; neither would they believe that I was instructed of the Lord." (1 Nephi 17:18.)

NOEL: Charles, you're ever more at home in the scriptures. It is even possible for people to believe but to lie. Listen to Alma: "Behold, I know that *thou believest, but thou art possessed with a lying spirit,* and ye have *put off the Spirit of God that it may have no place in you;* but the devil has power over you, and he doth carry you about, working devices that he may destroy the children of God." (Alma 30:42, italics added.) Note the eviction of the Spirit by providing *"no place* in you." This is the reverse side of Alma's words about accommodating the gospel seed "even until . . . ye can *give place* for a portion of my words." (Alma 32:27, italics added.) Sadly, it is also possible for a few people to prefer Satan, as we see in the Pearl of Great Price:

"Satan came among them, saying: I am also a son of God; and he commanded them, saying: Believe it not; and they believed it not, and they *loved Satan more than God.* And men began from that time forth to be carnal, sensual, and devilish." (Moses 5:13, italics added.)

Back to Jesus, and why He is such an exception even among prophets. These next marvelous verses, describing the youth of Jesus, came to us through Joseph Smith: "And it came to pass that Jesus grew up with his brethren, and waxed strong, and waited upon the Lord for the time of his ministry to come. And he served under his father, and he spake not as other men, neither could he be taught; for he needed not that any man should teach him. And after many years, the hour of his ministry drew nigh." (Matthew 3:24-26, JST; see also 1 John 2:20, 27.)

CHARLES: Those words "needed not that any man should teach him" . . . How set apart Jesus was from the very beginning!

NOEL: Ever at the center is Jesus and His remarkable atonement! The more one studies and ponders that gift of inestimable worth, the greater his awe and appreciation—the greater, too, his perspective, even in the midst of his own trials and tribulations.

May I suggest a stunning sample concerning which I cannot be definitive but concerning which I can still exult, exclaim, and be filled with gospel gladness? I refer to the hours that comprised Gethsemane and Calvary and the period just before!

CHARLES: Please go on.

NOEL: The enormous weight of the atonement Jesus began to feel confirmed His long-held intellectual understanding as to what He must do! In the temple,

Jesus' pleading began, His working through began: "Now is my soul troubled; and what shall I say? Father, save me from this hour: but for this cause came I unto this hour." (John 12:27.) The tension between compliance and avoidance must have been unimaginably intense! And this was not theater, was it? It was as real as anything ever was or could be!

We read how in Gethsemane Jesus began to be "sore amazed," or, according to the Greek, "astonished"! (Mark 14:33.) "Astonished," mind you. And this reaction from Him Who, among Father's spirit children, was and is "more intelligent than they all." (Abraham 3:19.) The Savior, with His unsurpassed brilliance, began to be "very heavy," or, again according to the Greek, "dejected" or "in anguish." (Mark 14:33.) Here we read of the Creator of this and other worlds, Who knew well beforehand what He must do. Nevertheless, Jesus had never before known personally the process of atonement. And it was much worse than even He in His brilliance had ever imagined! Listen to these verses: "He went forward a little, and fell on the ground, and prayed that, if it were possible, the hour might pass from him. And he said, Abba, Father, all things are possible unto thee; take away this cup from me: nevertheless not what I will, but what thou wilt." (Mark 14:35, 36.)

Jesus, once Jehovah, actually pled that the awful hour and the bitter cup might pass from Him. Note his special, significant words: "All things are possible unto thee; take away this cup from me."

CHARLES: Jesus taught this in His mortal ministry?

NOEL: He did, again and again! (See Matthew 19: 23-26; Mark 10:27; Luke 18:24-27.) Had not Jesus, as

Jehovah, said to Abraham, "Is anything too hard for the Lord?" (Genesis 18:14.) Had not an angel told a perplexed Mary concerning her own impending miracle as well as that of Elizabeth, "With God nothing shall be impossible"? (Luke 1:37.)

CHARLES: Even so, after this pleading came the sublime, unparalleled spiritual submissiveness: "Nevertheless not what I will, but what thou wilt." (Mark 14:36.) It is a wondrous and glorious moment of full submission in the act of the atonement.

NOEL: Who else has been as blessed as the Latter-day Saints with such added and affirming words as these concerning the atonement? "Lo, he shall suffer temptations, and pain of body, hunger, thirst, and fatigue, even more than man can suffer, except it be unto death; for behold, blood cometh from every pore, so great shall be his anguish for the wickedness and the abominations of his people." (Mosiah 3:7.)

Or consider these words from the resurrected Jesus himself confirming and describing the agony of the atonement: "Behold, I, God, have suffered these things for all, that they might not suffer if they would repent; but if they would not repent they must suffer even as I; which suffering caused myself, even God, the greatest of all, to tremble because of pain, and to bleed at every pore, and to suffer both body and spirit—and would that I might not drink the bitter cup, and shrink—nevertheless, glory be to the Father, and I partook and finished my preparations unto the children of men." (D&C 19:16-19.)

CHARLES: Yes . . . yes . . . and to whom else shall mortals go for such stunning truths? While we as Church members are the weak of the world—at least as the world measures strength—we are the Lord's messengers with the fullness of His gospel!

NOEL: And we must not forget Alma's special contribution as to how the atonement perfected Jesus' empathy since He thus came to know personally and perfectly "according to the flesh" what mortals bear as sicknesses and infirmities. (See Alma 7:11, 12.)

And if our souls would be stirred even more, we may think upon what the feelings might have been, at that hour, of the Father, who loved His Only Begotten Son with perfect love and with perfect empathy. The Father's role has not been fully revealed to us, but these words are full of portent and more truth than we can possibly manage: "Jesus answered them, My Father worketh *hitherto*, and I work. . . . Verily, verily, I say unto you, *The Son can do nothing of himself, but what he seeth the Father do:* for what things soever he doeth, these also doeth the Son likewise. For *the Father* loveth the Son, and *sheweth him all things that himself doeth:* and he will shew him greater works than these, that ye may marvel. (John 5:17-20, italics added.)

CHARLES: How wondrous to ponder! Dare we depart from declaring the central simplicity of Jesus' gospel? Is there anything else so wondrous and so sorely needed by mankind? So many puzzle over the meaning and purpose of life and over what lies beyond the grave. But there are answers to the ultimate questions, and these come to us from Christ.

NOEL: Therefore, Charles, unhesitatingly, "we talk of Christ, we rejoice in Christ, we preach of Christ, we prophesy of Christ, and we write . . . that our children may know to what source they may look." (2 Nephi 25:26.)

CHARLES: Noel, as I ponder what we have discussed, it puts me in mind of C. S. Lewis, who walked in the woods. Often he would be struck with what illumination a patch of sunlight could bring to a particular spot in the forest, "patches of God-light in the woods of our experience."[4] Today, Noel, needed light has come flooding into me, not in the woods, but in a small room in a busy cafe!

NOEL: You're right, such moments can occur in unlikely places—a lonely hospital room or a desolate battlefield. Or, as you implied, in the emptiness of a house that once knew better days and a wife's voice.

CHARLES: Thank you, Noel. It is so lonely at times, but solitude can have its uses. I sometimes wonder if, in fact, such moments are not designed precisely in order to focus us upon God—to show us our utter dependence on Him. Otherwise, the cares of the world will call the cadence.

NOEL: If life were merely lineal existence and all moments were of equal importance, then certain moments would not loom so large. But life is experiential, not lineal, isn't it? We have only to look at scriptural history to be reminded how often people's hearts must be softened by passing through hard times or hard experiences. Adversity is often present in those curricular clusters through which we pass.

CHARLES: Far better that we be humbled or even be brought down than that we be allowed to indulge ourselves to the everlasting detriment and destruction of our souls.

NOEL: How true. As I think of what you just said, I wonder about two scriptures that speak of a winnowing judgment that begins first with the house of God: "The time is come that judgment must begin at the house of God: and if it first begin at us, what shall the end be of them that obey not the gospel of God?" (1 Peter 4:17, see also D&C 112:24, 25.) These seem to suggest a time of winnowing and spiritual consolidation in the Church preceding or resulting from calamitous and stressful times in the world.

CHARLES: Then, we too may be required not only to tread our own tiny winepresses alone but also those larger winepresses we will face as a people? (D&C 76:107.)

NOEL: Apparently. But such circumstances can focus our faith so that it is not simply a vague expression of hope. As we all concluded several weeks ago, the faith required is so very different from a generalized hope about life.

CHARLES: We've talked before about the Light of Christ, Noel. Just how much illumination is there in individuals, each of whom is lighted by the light of Christ? (D&C 88:7-13.) I suppose we do not know. Furthermore, under what conditions, if any, is that light fully extinguished?

NOEL: When you phoned to say you wanted to discuss this topic, I researched that question and made copies of several quotations for you. First, from President George Q. Cannon: "We have the sweet influence of the Spirit of God pleading with us to do that which is right, pleading with every human being that does not drive it from him; for every human being has a portion of the Spirit of God given unto him. We sometimes call it conscience. . . . On the other hand, there is the influence of evil, the influence of the

Adversary enticing men to do wrong, . . . infusing doubt, infusing unbelief, infusing hardness of heart, infusing rebellion against everything that is holy and pure. We are all conscious of the existence of these two influences within us . . . one entreating to do right, the other enticing to do wrong, to commit sin and to violate the commandments of God."[5]

Next, from Wilford Woodruff: "The Holy Ghost . . . is different from the common Spirit of God, which we are told lighteth every man that cometh into the world. . . . This Spirit reveals, day by day, to every man who has faith, those things which are for his benefit. As Job says, 'There is a spirit in man and the inspiration of the Almighty giveth them understanding.' It is this inspiration of God to his children in every age of the world that is one of the necessary gifts to sustain man and enable him to walk by faith."[6]

Then, from Joseph F. Smith: "The Spirit of the Lord enlightens every man that comes into the world. There is no one that lives upon the earth, but what is, *more or less*, enlightened by the Spirit of the Lord Jesus. Without the light of the Spirit of Christ, no person can truly enjoy life. . . . There is not a man born into the world, but has a portion of the Spirit of God, and it is that Spirit of God which gives to his spirit understanding. Without this, he would be but an animal like the rest of the brute creation . . . but in proportion as he prostitutes his energies for evil, the inspiration of the Almighty is withdrawn from him, until he becomes so dark and so benighted, that so far as his knowledge of God is concerned, he is quite as ignorant as a dumb brute."[7]

Next, President J. Reuben Clark: "Every human being is born with the light of faith kindled in his heart as on an altar, and that light burns and the Lord sees that it burns, during the period before we are accountable. When accountability comes then each of us determines how we shall feed and care for that light. If we shall live righteously that light will glow until it suffuses the whole body, giving to it health and strength and spiritual light as well as bodily health. If we shall live unrighteously that light will dwindle and finally almost flicker out. Yet it is my hope and my belief that the Lord never permits the light of faith wholly to be extinguished in any human heart, however faint the light may glow. The Lord has provided that there shall still be there a spark which, with teaching, with the spirit of righteousness, with love, with tenderness, with example, with living the Gospel, shall brighten and glow again, however darkened the mind may have been."[8]

"God has placed in every man's heart a divine spark, which never wholly goes out; it may grow dim, it may become hidden, almost smothered by the ashes of transgression; but the spark still lives and glows and can be fanned into flame by faith, if the heart is touched."[9]

And, finally, President Harold B. Lee: "The only thing that will dim that light in you will be your own sinning that may render you insensible to its promptings and warnings as to right and wrong. It is a true saying that prayer keeps one from sin and that sin keeps one from prayer."[10]

CHARLES: Such powerful and reassuring quotations! Thanks for the copies. They help immensely to explain, don't they, why so many go on living decently, hoping and trusting, even in the midst of gross conditions and deep disbelief? They make reasonable the intrinsic goodness of so many mortals, the persistence of their hope, their honorable and correct behavior—even in the midst of so much wrong.

NOEL: Nor should we ever forget that Jesus has promised us the Comforter, the Holy Ghost, not only to give us guidance but to reassure us and to reinforce the reality of our relationship with the Father and Jesus. Furthermore, life's "key of knowledge" is "the fulness of the scriptures." (Luke 11:52, JST.)

CHARLES: I am so everlastingly grateful for what I have found in those precious pages of modern scripture, especially in view of all I have lost through an unwanted divorce. I try to be an effective father for our children even though they are all now married. Yet I feel so incomplete at times. I need help from so many. I pray for those married couples to have good home teachers. I found wry amusement in the story about the home teacher who was asked why he did not home teach twelve months a year instead of just ten; his indignant response was that he did not want to visit his families on Halloween and New Year's Eve!

NOEL: That's a new one, Charles! How fortunate that we, a linguist and a chemist, can engage, as today, in unashamedly "conversing about this Jesus Christ." (3 Nephi 11:2.)

CHARLES: I needed it! As you would know, since we both sit there representing different colleges, none of our topics today has been on an agendum of faculty council! We could have talked of the weather, legislation before Congress—the delectable but disappearing things of the day . . .

NOEL: Instead, for us today, it's been the things of eternity!

# Fourth Conversation:
# Attitudes toward Faith

"Though argument does not create conviction,
the lack of it destroys belief. . . . What no
one shows the ability to defend is quickly
abandoned. Rational argument does not create
belief, but it maintains a climate in which
belief may flourish."
(Austin Farrer, "The
Christian Apologist," p. 26.)

*The setting: Once again, the friends are meeting in Noel and Rachel's home. All are present, and the discussion concerns faith but particularly the challenges of living in a world in which the spectrum ranges from disbelief, to unbelief, to belief, to faith, and to knowledge, with people positioned at every point.*

---

NOEL: As we examine the different attitudes of people concerning faith, we quickly see that they are so spread out on the spectrum. A few, like Cain, actually love the devil more than the Lord. (Moses 5:28.) We see others, like Korihor, who know that certain spiritual truths are verifiable but who lie. (Alma 30:42.) We have others who are stubbornly skeptical, like those in Helaman's time. They said of fulfilled prophecies that any accuracy therein was to be accounted for simply because, among so many prophecies, the prophets merely guessed some right. (Helaman 16:16.)

RACHEL: Regrettably, too, there are others who have had spiritual experiences and have had prayers answered but who nevertheless adopt an attitude toward God of "What have you done for me lately?"

WINSTON: Rachel, I didn't know you were familiar with that political quip of Vice-President Alben Barkley about his constituents.

RACHEL: A leftover, Winston, from hearing a lecture long ago in political science. But just think of Laman and Lemuel! With all of their spiritual experiences, they had abundant evidence that God lives and hears and answers prayers.

CHARLES: Like ancient Israel, too, Rachel.

JEFFREY: Still others want to impose special conditions upon the Lord. Also in Helaman's time, some wanted Jesus to appear among them. Appearing back in Jerusalem, the land of their fathers, wouldn't do! (See Alma 46:8.)

NOEL: Then, too, Jeffrey, there are those like Nicodemus who genuinely and sincerely wonder about that which they have been told. Can a man enter again into the womb and be born again? (John 3:4.) And there are still others, like Gamaliel, who may not believe but who are not certain enough of their position to deride the truth.

WINSTON: The latter, at least, wanted his peers to keep their heavy hands off the work of the Lord. (Acts 5:34-36.)

RACHEL: Then there are those wonderful and worthy people, who, like the rich young man, are called but not chosen, because their hearts are so much set upon the things of this world! (See Mark 10:17-22.) They cannot, at the moment, fully follow Jesus without really committing to overcome a particular challenge or to develop in a particular way.

CHARLES: Are we back, again, to Alma's concept of developing faith in specific areas?

JEFFREY: We can't get away from it. Since our last discussion, I ran across this parallel statement by Brigham Young: "Every principle God has revealed carries its own convictions of its truth to the human mind."[1]

NOEL: It fits perfectly with Alma's assertion about how experimentation with each and every gospel principle can produce a knowledge of the truth, doesn't it. In fact, spiritual knowledge has its own system of verification. Jesus enunciated it: Do God's will and we will know if God's doctrines are true! (John 7:17.) The Lord Jesus did not wish people to think He was merely teaching His own doctrines.

CHARLES: Yet, Noel, if gospel ends are viewed by some either as undesirable or unattainable . . .

NOEL: And they are so viewed . . . Then, Charles, Jesus and His gospel will be seen by them as foolishness and irrelevance! Human fascination with human achievement has led some to narcissism in which there is no meekness whatsoever. Such individuals are unlikely to submit themselves to the rigors of obtaining spiritual knowledge, which require an ample supply of meekness.

WINSTON: Furthermore, if narcissism, as a way of life that excludes things spiritual, combines with sensualism in people's lifestyles, then there is little hope, for now, of reaching such people, I should think . . .

CHARLES: Those are hard sayings, Winston, that man's higher criticism of which some have grown so proud . . .

NOEL: Is part of the lower ways of man—precisely! (See Isaiah 55:9.) God's ways are higher than man's ways, and therefore man's methods can scarcely be used to verify God's ways.

But it is a hard doctrine, Charles. Man's ways are useful to explore man's realm, but these tools are too primitive for exploring a higher realm. But despite the seeming hardness of the gospel truths, I fail to see why the invitation in Alma—which is, in effect, to *arouse*, to *try*, and to *verify*—can be regarded as anything but a bold, open, yet practical invitation. The individual is still left to judge for himself, to come to know for himself!

CHARLES: Yet, Noel, as you yourself have pointed out, some of those who appear to be disbelievers are really believers still unwilling to come out into the open. (See John 12:42, 43.)

NOEL: Alas, so it is, Charles. Then, too, there are those like Amulek who are generally aware of the blessings of the Lord to His people but who are busy and preoccupied. These actually *know* and yet, at least for the moment, would *not know*. (Alma 10:5, 6.) Hence, they go on being preoccupied with the things of the world.

WINSTON: Now there's something we must discuss sometime—the cares of the world!

RACHEL: Yes, I agree! Marvelously, however, the gospel is able to respond to people in all of the circumstances just noted, wherever they are on the spectrum—disbelief, unbelief, belief, faith, or knowledge.

NOEL: Even if they have no more than a desire to believe. (Alma 32:27.) Perhaps skeptics demand evidence of things that can be seen because they are familiar only with the ways of man. God's ways and thoughts are higher than man's. (Isaiah 55:9.)

CHARLES: We mustn't be too judgmental of those so conditioned by the world.

NOEL: True. Such individuals, in a sense, do insist, however, upon continuing to use their water wings as a condition for entering the sea. God is saying, at some point, they must trust Him and cast off the water wings. No wonder some feel safest staying smugly on the secular shore, scorning those who have ventured forth "on the waves" to move toward Jesus.

JEFFREY: Then, too, Noel, we must make allowance for our premortal inclinations, including our previously developed capacity for faith, which we apparently brought with us. Alma chapter 13 is filled with portent in regard to this.

CHARLES: Be careful, or you'll be saying all is fixed by divine demographics.

JEFFREY: Good point, Charles. The elect hear the word of God wherever they are. The honest in heart do respond. However, it is left for us to proceed as if all mortals will hear, for they may choose to do so. After all, in the justice of God, each will have an on-the-record chance to have received the gospel *before* the judgment day, either on this side of the veil or the other.

WINSTON: Besides, how could we develop our love or humility if we were predestinarian in our views of other mortals? Such would produce a casualness, even a cavalierness, in our attitudes toward others.

NOEL: Again we are back to the importance of faith in Christ and in God's plan of salvation. This is the key to understanding the important role of such faith and the basis on which faith can move us into knowledge. Meanwhile, we need not denigrate the prized and highly useful scientific method or other mortal ways of learning. These are entirely appropriate for their realms. As a chemist, I'm genuinely grateful for the secular ways of discovering and knowing.

JEFFREY: There are some, however, who are so pre-occupied with secular knowledge that they despise the revelations of God and regard Jesus as a thing of naught. (1 Nephi 19:9.) Or consider Him a mere man. (Mosiah 3:9.) Or who consider the words of scripture as naught. (2 Nephi 33:2; Moses 1:41.)

NOEL: Alas, true, Jeffrey, and one searches almost in vain for analogies to describe the relationship of the spiritual and secular realms. Perhaps it is difficult because the gap between them is so real. Yet the truths in these realms are related.

CHARLES: But share with us anyway what you might have come up with, Noel.

NOEL: Well, at least lately, I've found this attempt at analogy to be somewhat useful. Someone afflicted with physical deafness could sit amid a symphony of sound but hear nothing, while those about him would

enjoy the thrill of great music. His would be an in-
voluntary deprivation, of course. One who is deaf to
spiritual sounds also sits unnoticing amid a different
kind of symphony. Yet the reality is likewise there,
since others, attuned, partake.

CHARLES: But the latter affliction is clearly voluntary!

PAULINE: Much like some of those in busy Jerusalem.
While Christ heard the voice of the Father, they heard
merely the sound of thunder. (John 12:29.)

NOEL: Precisely! For instance, too, Jesus once said, for
those who had "ears to hear," that John the Baptist
was an Elias. (Matthew 11:14, 15.) This statement was
of no small import, since John stirred things up consid-
erably, and there was apparently considerable speculation concerning John.

PAULINE: You're speaking of that deafness to spiritual
things that is "willed" by its victims. Paul said it would
happen, and on a large scale. Soon, some early Church
members turned away from sound doctrines, prefer-
ring fables to the truth. (2 Timothy 4:4.)

NOEL: Pauline is correct. This condition became general until the restoration, when, interestingly enough,
as ancient prophets said, the "deaf" would hear the
words of the Book of Mormon. (2 Nephi 27:29.)

CHARLES: But again, only those who choose for themselves to hearken?

NOEL: Only those, Charles. Thus, it is actually secularism, for reasons of its own, that is exclusionary,
not the Lord's Church, though the charge is made
otherwise. Jesus' promise of personal verification—do
God's will and thus know the truth of the doctrine—is
an open-ended invitation. (John 7:17.) But there is a

price to be paid and a process to be followed, neither of which can be waived. Therein is the stumbling block!

So it is not just the cares of the world that get in the way, but also the ways of the world, which contribute to the deafness. This is cause for cries of lamentation but not of discrimination.

WINSTON: Yet, ironically, we are put on guard against damage from noise pollution, a different kind of decibel level, aren't we?

PAULINE: Even shared experiences, however, do not guarantee shared beliefs, do they? There are those who receive the same teachings, side by side with believers, but who come out so differently—in attitude and lifestyle. These words are from Alma: "Now these dissenters, having the same instruction and the same information of the Nephites, yea, having been instructed in the same knowledge of the Lord, nevertheless, it is strange to relate, not long after their dissensions they became more hardened and impenitent, and more wild, wicked and ferocious than the Lamanites—drinking in with the traditions of the Lamanites; giving way to indolence, and all manner of lasciviousness; yea, entirely forgetting the Lord their God." (Alma 47:36.)

JEFFREY: It is always interesting to see the internal correlation of the prophets on any issue. When the light goes out . . . well, listen to what Joseph Smith said: "There is a superior intelligence bestowed upon such as obey the Gospel with full purpose of heart, which, if sinned against, the apostate is left naked and destitute of the Spirit of God. . . . When once that light which was in them is taken from them, they become as much darkened as they were previously enlightened, and then, no marvel, if all their power should be enlisted against the truth, and they, Judas like, seek the destruction of those who were their greatest benefactors."[2]

PAULINE: Yes. Furthermore, see how Joseph Smith correlates with Alma in yet another verse in Alma on this same topic: "After a people have been once enlightened by the Spirit of God, and have had great knowledge of things pertaining to righteousness, and then have fallen away into sin and transgression, they become more hardened, and thus their state becomes worse than though they had never known these things." (Alma 24:30.)

CHARLES: Perhaps those cynics who say, "Show to us a sign, and then we will believe," are not really demanding evidence as a condition of their belief as much as they are demanding that the whole experiment be performed on their terms!

WINSTON: It is God's invitation to us, isn't it? Not the other way around!

RACHEL: Besides, such a role reversal would invalidate God's whole plan of salvation. How can we surrender unconditionally unto the Lord if we are forever attaching conditions to our surrender?

NOEL: We can't, of course. Another touchingly candid and instructive episode concerning faith is found in these verses from Mark: "And they brought him unto him: and when he saw him, straightway the spirit tare him; and he fell on the ground, and wallowed foaming. And he asked his father, How long is it ago since this came unto him? And he said, Of a child. And ofttimes it hath cast him into the fire, and into the waters, to destroy him: but if thou canst do any thing, have compassion on us, and help us. Jesus said unto him, If thou canst believe, all things are possible to him that believeth. And straightway the father of the child cried out, and said with tears, Lord, I believe; help thou mine unbelief." (Mark 9:20-24.)

The anxious father believed and yet he pled for help with his remaining unbelief. This man believed in Jesus and in the miracles Jesus performed, but he needed faith with regard to the healing of his own stricken child.

RACHEL: This suggests, as in our previous discussions, how our faith can be too general. The other day in Relief Society, several older mothers commented about how our faith is particularly and specifically tested when the circumstances involve our children. For us, after all we can do, to "take it" as we watch our children "take it" is not easy. But we are not without example, for is that not, on a grand scale, what the Father did while His Only Begotten Son passed through the atonement?

PAULINE: Oh, Rachel, how I agree! It's so hard at times. Teaching early-morning seminary has sensitized me to how our youth must work out their salvation. But it's their parents who sometimes experience the "fear and trembling"!

NOEL: In fact, didn't Lehi once describe himself as a "trembling parent"? (2 Nephi 1:14.)

WINSTON: But back, please, to that fervent father. Ever since first reading the New Testament years ago on my mission, I have admired his tremendous candor and openness. He made as much of a declaration of belief as he honestly could, yet he realized how much more he needed to believe.

CHARLES: Perhaps it is important for us, too, to be candid not only with the Lord but with ourselves about how far our present belief or faith can take us. And we need to be fervent and genuine in pleading for divine help in order to extend and deepen our faith. But this requires our introspective honesty as a precondition, doesn't it?

WINSTON: Yes. Skimming over the surface of life and over the surface of the resplendent truths of the gospel can create the illusion that one is a believer and has adequate faith, when such may not be the case.

JEFFREY: Exactly. Almost like trying to survive only on what some Church members humorously call "faith-promoting rumors."

WINSTON: Superficial assent to general propositions will not do. To remain at that point, because of the lack of searching introspection, is an awful responsibility for any of us to bear. Instead, for us to plead for help with our unbelief is part of the lesson that flows from this episode of the fervent father.

NOEL: So once again we return to our recurring theme, my friends. The more our commitment to general propositions can be specific, the better! Surely this is part of what the thirty-second chapter of Alma is all about—planting the seed, patiently nourishing it, and watching it grow and sprout with regard to a particular principle, doctrine, or challenge to one's faith.

RACHEL: Even with accumulating knowledge, there will always be plenty of remaining realms in which faith can operate, won't there?

PAULINE: I agree. There will be ample acreage for each of us in which to plant more seeds—such as the need to have faith in how God's plans must affect our children but without seeking to immunize them from the challenges of life, even though we are striving to love, preserve, and protect them.

NOEL: However, nothing should cause us to hedge or to constrain our declarations or affirmations or testimonies to our children or others as to what we now actually do know or believe. Rather, we should be more open about the need to strengthen our faith. As such opportunities and experiences come along, we should see these as a reflection of God's love for us, not of any indifference toward us.

CHARLES: But some of our experiences that cause pain and that would have best been avoided occur because of our own stupidity, not divine design. Don't you agree?

NOEL: I do agree. Making mistakes, even innocently, is part of life's learning process, which involves developing our capacity to choose. And that's part of the divine design.

WINSTON: I'm struck again and again by how circumstances and social pressure can also keep the individual's faith from flowering fully and openly. Listen to these verses from Nephi: "After they had tasted of the fruit they were ashamed, because of those that were scoffing at them; and they fell away into forbidden paths and were lost." (1 Nephi 8:28.) Peer pressure through the ages!

JEFFREY: And changing circumstances can likewise affect nearly a whole people's faith, Winston. Listen to this verse: "There was not a living soul among all the people of the Nephites who did doubt in the least the

words of all the holy prophets who had spoken; for
they knew that it must needs be that they must be
fulfilled." (3 Nephi 5:1.)

Now, listen to this: "There began to be great doubtings and disputations among the people, notwithstanding so many signs had been given." (3
Nephi 8:4.)

As I check the years of these two verses, I note that
this decline happened in the space of a mere ten years
or less! Circumstances changed from one in which
"not a living soul" doubted the prophecies to a time in
which there were "great doubtings." It isn't very confidence inspiring, is it?

RACHEL: Apparently, for various reasons, some
ceased nourishing and tending the tree of testimony.
It withered. (See Alma 32:38.) We can be disappointed, but why should we be surprised? But it can
happen swiftly, as well as gradually, if the tree is un-
nourished.

NOEL: Yes, just as the process of growth of faith forms
and follows a pattern, so does the diminution of faith.

It's time to share any quotations, gems, tidbits, or
handouts you brought along.

JEFFREY: Alma's writing is so helpful. Listen: "There
are many who do say: If thou wilt show unto us a sign
from heaven, then we shall know of a surety; then we
shall believe. Now I ask, is this faith? Behold, I say
unto you, Nay; for if a man knoweth a thing he hath no
cause to believe, for he knoweth it." (Alma 32: 17, 18.)

I ran across something Brigham Young said that
parallels this. Wait a minute . . . here it is: "There is no
saving faith merely upon . . . acknowledging a fact."[3]

NOEL: Very germane. I would like to share this gem.
Elder James E. Talmage wrote: "Belief . . . may consist

in a merely intellectual assent, while faith implies such confidence and conviction as will impel to action. . . . Belief is in a sense passive, an agreement or acceptance only; faith is active and positive, embracing such reliance and confidence as will lead to works. Faith in Christ comprises belief in Him, combined with trust in Him. One cannot have faith without belief; yet he may believe and still lack faith. Faith is vivified, vitalized, living belief."[4]

"Knowledge is to wisdom what belief is to faith, one an abstract principle, the other a living application. Not possession merely, but the proper use of knowledge constitutes wisdom."[5]

WINSTON: How Elder Talmage's words hold up over the decades!

RACHEL: That's so true, Winston. I like what Elder Stephen L Richards said: "I admit that difficulties are to be encountered because a man cannot really know what faith is until he has experienced it, nor can he really experience it without recognizing it for what it is. It is rather confusing to say to one who denies the reality of spiritual things, "You, sir, cannot know what faith is because you have never had it and you cannot get it as long as you deny it." This sounds paradoxical, but in reality, it is not so absurd as it sounds, for this reason—faith is a divine gift open to all men to receive, if only their attitude and life will permit its reception. It is true only the faithful know this, but their knowledge of it is so certain that they never despair of bringing the knowledge to others. In this absolute certitude of the faithful lies the hope and promise of universal conversion."[6]

JEFFREY: Elder Richards's remarks are "fitly framed together" with those in John and Alma, aren't they? (See John 7:17; Alma 32.)

PAULINE: And I brought along the words of Elder Boyd K. Packer: "There was a test of faith involved, as the Lord asked: 'Believest thou the words which I *shall* speak?' (Ether 3:11. Italics added.) Interesting, isn't it, that he was not asked, 'Believest thou the words that I *have* spoken?' It didn't relate to the past. It related to the future. The brother of Jared was asked to commit himself on something that had not yet happened. He was to confirm his belief in that which the Lord had not yet spoken. . . . Faith, to be faith, must center around something that is not known. Faith, to be faith, must go beyond that for which there is confirming evidence. Faith, to be faith, must go into the unknown. Faith, to be faith, must walk to the edge of the light, and then a few steps into the darkness. If everything has to be known, if everything has to be explained, if everything has to be certified, then there is no need for faith. Indeed, there is no room for it."[7]

WINSTON: "To the edge of the light, and then a few steps into the darkness." I like that! In a way, nonbelievers are too afraid of the dark, aren't they!

CHARLES: Darkness can consist, at the moment, of whatever is unknown or not fully fathomed by us, can't it?

NOEL: Yes. Even for Jesus. He knew intellectually what the atonement would require of Him, yet He still had never personally experienced the anguish of an atonement. Even before Gethsemane and Calvary, He felt the approaching agony. Ponder His plea in the temple after His triumphal entry into Jerusalem: "Now is my soul troubled; and what shall I say? Father, save me from this hour: but for this cause came I unto this hour." (John 12:27.)

It is so touching, even at our incomprehending level, to see the stern requirements of divine duty meeting the understandable human hope to avoid what lay ahead.

JEFFREY: I must have skimmed over that powerful scripture, Noel. It is so helpful to the understanding of Jesus' later words, isn't it? "O my Father, if it be possible, let this cup pass from me: nevertheless not as I will, but as thou wilt." (Matthew 26:39.)

RACHEL: Yes, Jeffrey, especially if we read these words of King Benjamin's concerning that awful but glorious moment: "Lo, he shall suffer temptations, and pain of body, hunger, thirst, and fatigue, even more than man can suffer, except it be unto death; for behold, blood cometh from every pore, so great shall be his anguish for the wickedness and the abominations of his people." (Mosiah 3:7.)

PAULINE: Especially, too, if we read Mark's version of that unique pleading in which, as only He could have, Jesus pleaded and invoked: "He said, Abba, Father, all things are possible unto thee; take away this cup from me: nevertheless not what I will, but what thou wilt." (Mark 14:36.)

CHARLES: Noel and I talked of these verses recently. Jesus wondered if an omniscient and omnipotent Father might, after all, have another way. Yet there was Jesus' ultimate submission: "nevertheless." Then Jesus went a few steps into the dark, trusting, submitting as He entered upon what was, for Him, as Noel said, a totally new experience! Oh, the eloquence of His example!

WINSTON: I share Charles's sense of awe.

My gem comes from practical and spiritual President Joseph Fielding Smith: "Faith in Christ and Joseph Smith go together. By faith we come to God. If we did not believe in the Lord Jesus Christ, if we had no faith in him or in his atonement, we would not be inclined to pay any heed to his commandments. It is because we have that faith that we are brought into harmony with his truth and have a desire in our hearts to serve him. . . .

"The first principle of the gospel is faith in the Lord Jesus Christ; and of course we are not going to have faith in the Lord Jesus Christ without having faith in his Father. Then if we have faith in God the Father and the Son and are guided, as we ought to be, by the Holy Ghost, we will have *faith in the servants of the Lord* through whom he has spoken.

"We must have faith in the mission of Joseph Smith. Because the world had lapsed into spiritual darkness, changed the ordinances and broken the everlasting covenant, the Church of Jesus Christ had to be brought again from the heavens. *Where there is no faith in these truths, there is no faith in Jesus Christ who sent the Prophet Joseph Smith.* This knowledge is vital to our eternal salvation."[8]

May I say, too, how I particularly appreciate to-night's and our previous discussions on faith. Our faith is to be brought to bear in certain moments on particular things. It is these moments that can increase the quality and depth of our faith.

NOEL: Well said, Winston. Operational faith, therefore, is like operational revelation. Operational faith is more focused than generalized faith. In the same way, individual operational revelation is a somewhat different thing from doctrinal revelation given to the Church in its entirety.

PAULINE: Please elaborate, Noel.

NOEL: Operational revelation usually has to do with the *who, how,* and *when* of human conduct and decision making as distinguished from doctrinal revelation, which has to do with *what* and *why.*

Operational faith has to do with proceeding from a basic faith that God lives and that He has given us commandments as to how we, in a particular situation, should comply with the need for obedience.

Faith is thus built experience by experience, line upon line, precept upon precept as the Lord leads us along. (Isaiah 28:10, 13; D&C 50:40.) We can know that He lives but still need to know that His scriptures are true. We can know that He loves his children but still need to know that He loves us personally and perfectly, especially at a particularly needful moment.

WINSTON: Noel, what you just said is especially illuminating for me.

CHARLES: For us all! Discussing faith *does* help.

NOEL: God is not a passive presence somewhere in space. He is our tutoring Lord and Shepherd. We can better handle a "no" answer to our prayers if we know those prayers are nevertheless heard by such a loving and living God. However, it is not possible for us to so trust if we are uncertain as to whether or not He is even there—or as to what kind of God He is!

How fortunate we are to have the scriptures, which were designed not only to tell us that God and Jesus live but what They are like and what Their purposes are!

JEFFERY: Can we discuss petitionary prayer next time?

NOEL: We'll be at your home, Jeffrey; it's up to you.

PAULINE: Sounds fine! Bear with one last word from me, please. Though God always meters out life's challenges so that they don't exceed our ability to cope, there may be times and seasons, mightn't there, when, from our standpoint we feel we are encountering a fire-hydrant's torrent of tribulation?

WINSTON: Yes, Pauline! And then, unless we have more than belief, our belief can break down under such pressures—unless, like the candid father, we invite the Lord's help. Then our belief can be strengthened.

CHARLES: Likewise, little faith, before long, can give way to doubt.

NOEL: But we can develop unshakable faith, as did several prophets. (Enos 1:11; Jacob 7:5.) Small faith can grow; it can be toughened and tempered. It will not, however, grow in the abstract, nor in the absence of the relevant experiences. We cannot mature our faith without these. There is no other way.

RACHEL: And because life is so filled with fresh experiences, we can never get very far, nor should we try to, from faith as an operating principle in our lives.

NOEL: Perhaps the need to develop faith about the basics is one of the reasons why we are warned about the mysteries, what might be called the radioactive doctrines. We are ready to experiment, as Alma urged, with basic gospel principles, but we are ill-equipped to handle the radioactive doctrines in the tiny laboratories of our minds; they can become a dangerous diversion from what our highest priority really is—to become like Jesus! (Matthew 5:48; 3 Nephi 27:27.)

WINSTON: Excellent, Noel! Jesus' direction to us—in Matthew 5:48—to become like the Father was, after all, so bold . . .

NOEL: Yes. And we have no indication that it was dismissed as unpardonable arrogance by the disciples. They did not challenge "that thing" as an impossible objective.

JEFFREY: The need for such emulation has been taught in various ways, in various times, and by various individuals after Jesus' mortal ministry. But setting forth such a historical verification would take a whole evening.

RACHEL: But how worthwhile, Jeffrey!

WINSTON: How we depend, in this quest, not only on the Lord to nourish our faith, but upon each other! Sadly, in our busyness, we sometimes fail other members of the Church.

CHARLES: Yes, Winston. Sometimes we are, in our busyness, like the sincere but unnoticing hospital visitor who stood on the patient's oxygen tube while anxiously inquiring about the patient's welfare!

# Fifth Conversation:
# The Plan of Salvation

"The great God has had mercy on us,
and made these things known unto us that we
might not perish; yea, and he has made
these things known unto us beforehand,
because he loveth our souls as well as he
loveth our children; therefore, in his mercy
he doth visit us by his angels, that the
plan of salvation might be made known unto
us as well as unto future generations."
(Alma 24:14.)

*The setting: The friends are gathered in the home of Jeffrey and Pauline. The lesson concerns the plan of salvation and the need for specific faith in the divine design that undergirds and pervades that plan.*

---

JEFFREY: One of the reasons Pauline phoned all of you ahead of time with changed reading assignments was our decision to move topically somewhat away from our schedule, at least temporarily. The previous discussions on faith seemed to lead so naturally into tonight's topic, the plan of salvation. Please go ahead, Pauline, with the introduction.

PAULINE: One of the great but underappreciated blessings flowing from confirming and amplifying Latter-day revelations is the crucial doctrinal framework of the great plan of salvation (Alma 42:5), the plan of happiness (Alma 42:8), or the plan of mercy (Alma 42:15). Whatever its designation, it represents, as Alma wrote, the redeeming and "great plan of the Eternal God." (Alma 34:9.) What the Holy Bible teaches, modern scriptures both amplify and confirm.

JEFFREY: Though the plan is sometimes treated too casually—

CHARLES: Casually! Sometimes less spiritually than diagrammatically, such as on the chalkboard in a class I attended recently—more like a floor plan than a grand plan of salvation!

JEFFREY: The plan, nevertheless, represents a striking, even stunning, example of the precious perspective the gospel of Jesus Christ gives to mortals! In fact, genuine faith in the Lord Jesus Christ includes and requires faith in His Father's plan of salvation.

NOEL: Rachel helped me to see that more clearly awhile back, Jeffrey. Since then, I'm persuaded that if one stays or strays outside this revealed framework of understanding, he or she risks developing provincial attitudes and destructive behavior.

JEFFREY: Exactly. Forgive me, but human misery is nothing more than the flip side of the Ten Commandments. Most of the news we read or watch on television represents, in one way or another, the breeching of God's commandments, departures from the "great plan of our God." Different consequences emerge so quickly from different lifestyles. Pauline . . .

PAULINE: First, there is in human nature a fixed tendency to please oneself and for each person to walk in his own selfish way. Unchecked, this tendency brings unhappiness. (D&C 1:16.)

CHARLES: And there is another fact that some won't acknowledge—that belief in immortality and in our individual accountability are much more intertwined than most realize, so far as human behavior is concerned.

JEFFREY: Indeed. Second, there is a human tendency to seek sensations. But sensations can obscure our true obligations; they represent "now" and seem so real.

PAULINE: Third, if one tends to regard others as functions and not as everlasting individual entities, he will seek as few lasting and obligating relationships as possible. Doing this, ironically, ensures less and less happiness and even further deterioration in the total human environment. Yet, today, more and more people seek to travel through life selfishly, as unencumbered and uncommitted as possible.

JEFFREY: Fourth, the possibility is high that sooner or later such an individual will feel despair and hopelessness as he contemplates life, saying wistfully, if not bitterly, "Is this all there is? Why should I behave?" Sadly, those possessed of such hopelessness sometimes denigrate those who do have a brightness of hope and spiritual certitude. I encounter such feelings on the part of some in the business world. Sometimes, however, in those rare moments when business associates who do not enjoy the gospel let their hair down, they talk about their innermost feelings. I'm surprised to see their doubts about their doubts.

CHARLES: Jeffrey, I occasionally hear counterpart conversations on the campus among colleagues!

In terms of truths most needed by mortals, God's plan of salvation assures us that mortality is not a conclusive and massive mausoleum, does it not?

PAULINE: It does, and that is a reassurance so desperately needed.

RACHEL: In fact, this planet is a garden to be dressed!

CHARLES: Trust Rachel to put things in such a positive perspective.

WINSTON: In legal terms, God's plan of salvation puts this planet to its "highest and best use."

NOEL: I'm impressed that an ancient prophet was told emphatically by the Lord to teach the vital fundamentals of this plan freely. (Moses 6:58, 62.) And ever at the center of it all is Jesus, who is our Best Friend and who will return to where He was once wounded by His friends. (Zechariah 13:6; D&C 45:51-53.) He is the Implementor of His Father's plan of happiness in which he "doeth not anything save it be for the benefit of the world." (2 Nephi 6:24.) He labors, lovingly and constantly as Moses declared, "for our good always." (Deuteronomy 6:24.)

PAULINE: I'm impressed with how seminary students seem to appreciate especially the Lord's familiar declaration of His grand design: "This is my work and my glory—to bring to pass the immortality and eternal life of man." (Moses 1:3.) It is so reassuring to them! To us all. But I wonder how often the plan is discussed effectively and lovingly in their homes.

RACHEL: And is it discussed in terms of how it shows God's love for us? Even when we learn to love God, as we contemplate His plan, we must acknowledge that He loved us *first*. (1 John 4:19.)

CHARLES: As you talk of the plan of salvation, it seems that Shakespeare was not very wide of the mark in writing, "All the world's a stage."[1] But it is not for play acting!

WINSTON: The very word *"plan"* connotes Paternal and Providential purpose, doesn't it? How desperately an understanding of that plan is needed in today's confused and despairing world!

JEFFREY: Exactly, Winston. The "plan of happiness" ensures us not only a perpetuation of our individual identity but also of glorious outcomes and of added reasons for endless rejoicing.

NOEL: Meanwhile, the spreading misery is caused by the adversary, whose desire is to have all mortals become miserable like unto himself. (2 Nephi 2:27.) He selfishly preferred his ascendancy to our agency. To him, meekness is weakness and sensuous pleasure is joy.

PAULINE: So true. The adversary works against the purposes of the plan. Fittingly, one insightful and grateful prophet said, "O how great the plan of our God." (2 Nephi 9:13.)

JEFFREY: And yet another prophet exclaimed, "The great God has had mercy on us, and made these things known unto us that we might not perish . . . because he loveth our souls . . . ; therefore, in his mercy he doth visit us by his angels, that the plan of salvation might be made known unto us." (Alma 24:14.)

WINSTON: And where would we be, my friends, without visits in our time by angels who taught us anew about this plan?

NOEL: Winston is right; without modern revelation, we'd be poorly informed indeed. In our rejoicing regarding the overall plan, it is sobering to realize that the mortal portion of God's grand plan is so precisely designed. It is what one would and should expect to experience in a deliberately constructed proving and tutoring experience. There is, now, no way *around*; the only way to go is *through*!

CHARLES: Yes! And what a "through" it is!

NOEL: Even amid sin, however, there is hope for the contrite. Listen to these verses: "All his transgressions that he hath committed, they shall not be mentioned unto him: in his righteousness that he hath done he shall live." (Ezekiel 18:22.)

"Come now, and let us reason together, saith the Lord: though your sins be as scarlet, they shall be as white as snow; though they be red like crimson, they shall be as wool." (Isaiah 1:18.)

PAULINE: I recite again, "O how great the plan of our God!" (2 Nephi 9:13.) In all dimensions!

NOEL: A justified encore, Pauline. This plan of mercy not only provides place for error but also for growth by recognition and redress of error, for the resumption of interrupted individual development. Provision is made for a brave Peter faltering and sinking on the

churning waves—and yet crying out "Lord, save me."
(Matthew 14:30.) For a Moses struggling with the bur-
dens of leadership and people fatigue. (See Numbers
11:11, 14, 29.) For a Jonah to crave Tarshish but still to
reach Nineveh, thereby receiving a great lesson in
compassion. For erring Oliver Cowdery, Martin Har-
ris, and Thomas B. Marsh, later in their lives, to vote
with their feet by traveling westward in reconciliation
to sustain the plan and its enunciating prophets.

WINSTON: Sometimes our finest hours occur during
or following our darkest hours, don't they? Not only
are whole peoples "in process of time," but individuals are "in process of time," like unfinished, un-
sculptured pieces of marble or an emerging canvas! In
fact, as my teenage daughter reminded me the other
day, in that trite but true phrase, "God is not finished
with her yet."

NOEL: It is an incredible irony, isn't it, that some com-
plainingly use these very tutoring and soul-shaping
arrangements of the Lord against Him? Or resent the
reality that we are to walk by faith during this mortal
experience?

RACHEL: Or resent the necessity of death. There must
be exit routes. We cannot, even by faith, block all these
exits all the time and for all people, can we?

CHARLES: Rachel, your faith is as practical as it is precious! Some also resent the fact that this mortal experience is also designed so that previous recollections are
withheld. Hence, at this moment, we do not see the
end from the beginning. But God does. Meanwhile,
we are in that "murky middle."

PAULINE: Even in the "murky middle" we can still
know that God loves us individually and perfectly,

though we cannot always explain the meaning of all things happening to us or around us. (1 Nephi 11:17.)

JEFFREY: Sometimes I feel so enclosed by time and the veil. We truly are tightly locked into this cocoon, this mortal classroom. We would be totally provincial in outlook except for faith in and knowledge of God's emancipating plan. How vital, therefore, is faith in the "great plan of the Eternal God" as well as faith in Jesus, the Finisher of that salvation! (Hebrews 12:2.)

PAULINE: You can see why Jeffrey and I wanted to discuss this topic as a part of our discussions of faith! The truths in this plan are not a matter of abstract theology. They can help us, materially and constantly, with regard to daily life. These perspectives from the plan are crucial to how we see ourselves, others, the Lord, life, and even the universe. Or how we view a baby. Or death. Or how we regard the praise and honors of men.

NOEL: I'm so grateful for the Restoration, for the light of the gospel that has broken forth to dispel darkness. (See D&C 45:28.) It is by this light that we can thus see everything else, including our place in Father's unfolding plan of salvation. This plan is truly the mother lode of meaning. It can cradle us, conceptually, amid any concern.

JEFFREY: Beautiful, Noel! Hence, the urgency of the restoration of Christ's doctrines pertaining to the plan of salvation!

NOEL: In fact, Jeffrey, the revelations concerning the plan stand like sentinel scriptures to mark and light the way for man. The gospel guardrails that line the strait and narrow path are there to guide us, nudge us, and even to jar us for the sake of our spiritual safety!

CHARLES: Without an understanding of God's plan of salvation, however, life makes little or no sense. With such an understanding, the reaching, the striving, the suffering, and the tutoring and enduring experiences of life play their part in the intelligible process of helping us to become, as the Savior beckoningly invited, "even as I am." (3 Nephi 27:27.)

RACHEL: Yet, as someone noted already, there are individuals who would use the very simplicity of God's plan against Him, who complain about its plainness.

NOEL: How true! Still others are willing to surrender superficially to God, but only on their terms—as if there could be conditions attached to unconditional surrender.

JEFFREY: As said so many times before in this group, faith is not merely to have a general hope but to have a particular faith, including faith in God's plan of salvation.

NOEL: True, Jeffrey! Such faith then admits one to the interior of the plan of happiness wherein awaits a wonder world of felicity and consistency.

CHARLES: Even so, Noel, it seems that the plan, with all its consistency, may not appeal to anyone whose life is inconsistent. Nor will it enfold him who is too worried about being taken in. It has no place of honor for him who is too concerned with losing his place in the secular synagogue. (John 12:42, 43.)

The plan reflects a caring Father and a redeeming Savior, but believers in it are not automatically immune to the cares of the world, are they?

WINSTON: Hmmm. The plan also places tremendous emphasis on human agency, but it may also reflect our previous agreements now forgotten but freely made!

The plan points the way, but it does not always smooth the way. Oh, how there are times when I wish, provincially, of course, that in individual development there did not need to be "opposition in all things." (2 Nephi 2:11.)

PAULINE: Don't we all!

WINSTON: Of all the errors mortals could make, God's plan of salvation is the wrong thing to be wrong about, isn't it?

NOEL: No error could be more enormous or more everlasting in its consequences. Yet this plan features generosity, not exclusivity. Even now, our Redeemer, who implemented God's plan of mercy, waits for us with open arms. (Mormon 6:17.)

No wonder the Lord wants the plan taught in its simplicity, uncluttered by vain mortal musings—in its plainness and without mystifications. It is challenging enough to walk by faith without attempts to add to the full field pack we mortals carry. Besides, it is God's plan—not ours!

WINSTON: And given the unimpressive outcomes of mortal secular plans to solve the world's problems, aren't we glad!

CHARLES: Yet we are still free to choose for ourselves. (2 Nephi 2:27.)

NOEL: And Nephi's words are underscored, Charles, by these words in the book of Moses: "nevertheless, thou mayest choose for thyself." (Moses 3:17.) God's gift of moral agency tells us so much that is wonderful about His beneficial purposes, doesn't it? But our misuse and abuse of that agency tells us awful things about ourselves! Unsurprisingly, this mortal school, constructed to help us overcome our frailties, creates a history replete with mistakes. But we should not blame the school! Nor the curriculum! Least of all, the Schoolmaster!

Besides, finishing schools have a way of knocking off the rough edges. So the debris of our deficiencies, the morass of our mistakes, is of our own making, like tailings around a mine or litter in a nursery.

WINSTON: An apt analogy, Noel!

JEFFREY: Remember, God has given each mortal the "Light of Christ." (D&C 93:2.) By that means He prompts us but refuses to intimidate us. Though such reminders usually go unheeded, the record will be clear—a loving God tried!

PAULINE: God gladly credits in the book of life (Revelation 20:12) all our goodness and service. At that moment of perfect judgment, realization, and recognition, all will acknowledge not only that Jesus is the Christ but that God's judgment and justice are perfect! (Alma 12:15.)

CHARLES: Including those who were unconvinced, those who were eager to believe the worst, and those who ignored their wild doubts of doubt all along the way.

WINSTON: No wonder this Church and its people go to such great lengths and expense to share the fulness of the gospel! No wonder the full gospel of Jesus Christ is such glorious and "good news"! I'm so glad I have a missionary son so contributing.

RACHEL: You'll miss his letters when he comes home, Winston!

NOEL: Meanwhile, discipleship in the last days is to be no picnic in the park. As Church members, we must come to terms with events in these, our days. Scriptural phrases from former periods of stress such as "great doubtings" (3 Nephi 8:4), "a great uproar" (3 Nephi 1:5-7), and disputations may yet come to have more meaning. But all will be well! The Lord will lead his people along.

Ponder this reassurance: "Great tribulations shall be among the children of men, but my people will I preserve." (Moses 7:61.) Those who have endured—but only with much murmuring—will, one day see the smallness of their causes and the faithlessness of their complaints.

PAULINE: Like the murmuring of those followers who complained because Nephi broke his bow (1 Nephi 16:18-22) or because Nephi was not thought able to build a ship (1 Nephi 17:17-19). These may have their modern equivalents.

CHARLES: The adversary, with his immense ego and selfish pride, understands so well, doesn't he, the uses to which swollen egos can be put? After all, doctrinal apostasy is not necessary if, as with Thomas Marsh, arguments over milk strippings will do!

PAULINE: Yes! Similarly, those who have endured well and whose souls have been stretched will understand better the causes of attrition in the march of Zion's camp and admire its spiritual survivors all the more.

JEFFREY: There will be more empathy, too, with Elisha's young servant who feared because of encirclement by the outnumbering enemy. He sought solace from the prophet, who told him, "Fear not, for they that be with us are more than they that be with them." But the young man could count and it did not look that way to him—until, after the prophet's prayer, the young man's eyes were opened and he saw "the mountain . . . full of horses and chariots of fire." (2 Kings 6:16-17.)

NOEL: We may even come to appreciate more, too, the lesson taught ancient Israel when thousands of warriors were rejected in favor of only 300 warriors who, under Gideon, triumphed. All of which was done "lest Israel vaunt themselves," thinking that they, not the Lord, provided the victory! (Judges 7:2.)

PAULINE: All of your comments have been so helpful, especially in showing how, in the midst of "all these things," events and circumstances will help more and more Church members to get a witness for themselves that this work is true.

CHARLES: Something that should have been done anyway! The plan puts both goodness and sinfulness into a practical perspective, it seems to me.

WINSTON: In that regard, Noel, I seem to recall your mentioning to us, that you've wondered if sin doesn't reflect a form of temporary insanity. Could you elaborate on that for us?

NOEL: I have said something like that. It's been an observation almost forced upon me, especially after someone who knows better commits a major transgression that surprises and disappoints.

I don't mean to suggest any lack of accountability, just that the words like *darkness* that the scriptures repeatedly use to describe sin seem to fit so well with what actually happens. For instance, if one who commits adultery could see beforehand all the consequences that would flow from that act, would he still do it? I doubt it, at least much of the time. It's when the light that would illuminate loyalties and consequences departs that such sins occur. As an individual thinks only of the moment and the immediate desires for gratification, selfish and self-pitying feelings dominate. It's as if wife, children, job, and, most of all, the Lord, did not—for the moment—count for anything!

WINSTON: I suppose we've all heard victims of that sort of situation say later on that they didn't realize how they could have done such a thing, something so out of character for them. Perhaps it is only in such darkness that the adversary can market his goods; they cannot be sold if viewed in the full light of the day.

NOEL: Again, I stress that even though there is such darkness, which blots out what might have been deterrents, the individual is still accountable. In fact, the record will be clear that the individual willed to do what he did. Furthermore, sometimes, in a step-by-step process of involvement, the erring individual has consciously moved ever more deeply into the darkness.

CHARLES: And darkness has a way of not calling attention to its own intensification!

NOEL: Aptly put, Charles. In any event, the relationship of light to truth and happiness is clear, as is the relationship of darkness to sin and unhappiness.

CHARLES: As you spoke, Noel, I thought, too, of how the spiritual radiance from a righteous man or woman is an almost physical thing. Luminosity is its own witness, isn't it?

JEFFREY: This evening demonstrates how the discussion of the gospel can be so stimulating. I've often wondered how that sense of excitement must have been felt by those in the Prophet Joseph's day—at the front end of this dispensation when the newness as well as the fulness of the gospel was so in evidence. Pauline found an amusing anecdote that may serve as a concluding illustration of the excitement of those early days.

PAULINE: It is not profound, merely indicative. Much as I wish Jeffrey enjoyed gardening and also had the time to do it . . . I'm becoming a little philosophical about it. Just as, for different reasons, Emma Smith reportedly became philosophical about her husband's erratic efforts at gardening. We found this quotation from Emma in a later comment to one of her children: "I do not expect you can do much more in the garden than your father could, and I never wanted him to go into the garden to work for if he did it would not be fifteen minutes before there would be three or four or sometimes a half dozen men round him and they would tramp the ground down faster than he could hoe it up."[2]

RACHEL: That is a precious anecdote, Pauline. But this whole evening has been precious. All of us thank you and Jeffrey so much.

# Sixth Conversation: Spiritual Knowledge

"In faith we plant the seed, and soon we see the miracle of the blossoming. Men have often misunderstood and have reversed the process. They would have the harvest before the planting, the reward before the service, the miracle before the faith."
(Spencer W. Kimball,
*Faith Precedes the Miracle*, p. 4.)

*The setting:* *A winter evening in the home of Jeffrey and Pauline. All are present and have come prepared after completing assigned readings on the nature and importance of spiritual knowledge.*

---

JEFFREY: The quest for spiritual knowledge is a call to an incredible adventure. This adventure is anything but easy. It is not for the unmotivated or the uncurious. It is not for the desensitized or for the satisfied and preoccupied, whose reaction to the gospel often is as described by John, who had encountered those who said, in effect, "I am rich, and increased with goods, and have need of nothing." (Revelation 3:17.)

PAULINE: I agree. Obtaining spiritual knowledge is, in fact, not a mechanical process at all. It is a journey of discovery, a step-by-step struggle.

NOEL: Pauline, that is so true. Enos described the laboriousness of one of his experiences: "I will tell you of the wrestle which I had before God, before I received a remission of my sins. Behold, I went to hunt beasts in the forests; and the words which I had often heard my father speak concerning eternal life, and the joy of the saints, sunk deep into my heart. And my soul hungered; and I kneeled down before my Maker, and I cried unto him in mighty prayer and supplication for mine own soul; and all the day long did I cry unto him; yea, and when the night came I did still raise my voice high that it reached the heavens. And there came a voice unto me, saying: Enos, thy sins are forgiven thee, and thou shalt be blessed. And I, Enos, knew that God could not lie; wherefore, my guilt was swept away." (Enos 1:2-6.)

CHARLES: I love that phrase "eternal life, and the joy of the saints"!

JEFFREY: It is filled with implications, isn't it? In any event, the insights and truths, the blessings to be realized in this adventure, come after hungering and wrestling and by strict obedience to specific spiritual laws. Consider these verses: "There is a law, irrevocably decreed in heaven before the foundations of this world, upon which all blessings are predicated—and when we obtain any blessing from God, it is by obedience to that law upon which it is predicated." (D&C 130:20, 21.)

NOEL: Those words parallel another scripture. Forgive me, Jeffrey and Pauline, but do you recall how truths are apparently independently "packaged" or placed in the structure of things? Perhaps, therefore, they must be independently extracted? Listen to this verse: "All truth is independent in that sphere in which God has placed it, to act for itself, as all intelligence also; otherwise there is no existence." (D&C 93:30.)

PAULINE: Frankly, I'd never thought of that, Noel.

JEFFREY: In any event, this adventure into the realm of spiritual knowledge involves rigorous behaving as well as rigorous learning. In fact, behaving facilitates knowing, as Peter declared: "If these things be in you, and abound, they make you that ye shall neither be barren nor unfruitful in the knowledge of our Lord Jesus Christ." (2 Peter 1:8.)

RACHEL: But Peter also spoke of the provincialism of the unspiritual, the nearsightedness of the unbelieving. Listen: "But he that lacketh these things is blind, and cannot see afar off, and hath forgotten that he was purged from his old sins." (2 Peter 1:9.)

PAULINE: Yes, Rachel, and the Spirit gives us not only breadth but depth also: "God hath revealed them unto us by his Spirit: for the Spirit searcheth all things, yea, the deep things of God. For what man knoweth the things of a man, save the spirit of man which is in him? Even so the things of God knoweth no man, but the Spirit of God. (1 Corinthians 2:10, 11.)

JEFFREY: In a way, the world of the Spirit has its own language, symbols, and requirements. But I'm getting onto your turf, Charles. I'd best leave things pertaining to language symbols up to you.

Also, the Spirit brings special liberating benefits. Paul wrote, "Now . . . where the Spirit of the Lord is, there is liberty." (2 Corinthians 3:17.)

NOEL: A different liberty, Jeffrey, than the false freedom Cain reported: "Cain gloried in that which he had done, saying: I am free; surely the flocks of my brother falleth into my hands." (Moses 5:33.)

JEFFREY: Exactly! The following seemed to Pauline and me to be among the ways in which spiritual knowledge can be acquired. Pauline . . .

PAULINE: First, our intellects are to be vigorously and constantly involved. We are to study problems out in our mind, not lazily or superficially. The Lord said to Oliver Cowdery, "Behold, you have not understood; you have supposed that I would give it unto you, when you took no thought save it was to ask me." (D&C 9:7.)

Then subsequent spiritual confirmation can come. This is one of the ways: "But, behold, I say unto you, that you must study it out in your mind; then you must ask me if it be right, and if it is right I will cause that your bosom shall burn within you; therefore, you shall feel that it is right." (D&C 9:8.)

JEFFREY: Second, acquiring spiritual knowledge may be accelerated by fasting and praying, as did Alma. He "fasted and prayed many days" in order to know. (See Alma 5:46.)

PAULINE: Third, at least Jeffrey and I have concluded, spiritual knowledge involves a special form of humility. As the eyes of our understanding are opened wider, our understanding of certain things will become restructured. This can be hard on one's mind and pride.

RACHEL: Pauline, I'm glad you said that! It has seemed to me that pride can be such a deterrent to spiritual knowledge. Intellectual humility makes room for revelation, which can bring entirely new knowledge to man. For instance, the reality of the resurrection, quite understandably, was a puzzling concept even to some of the faithful.

NOEL: Furthermore, opinion preceded revelation concerning the resurrection in yet another way, as noted in Alma: "My son, I do not say that their resurrection cometh at the resurrection of Christ; but behold, I give it as my opinion, that the souls and the bodies are reunited, of the righteous, at the resurrection of Christ, and his ascension into heaven." (Alma 40:20.)

WINSTON: Hmmm! How similar to another episode about which my missionary son wrote the other day, calling these verses to my attention.

May we read together in Third Nephi, chapter twenty eight? One ancient prophet who encountered translated beings had similar uncertainty—at least initially. He progressed, however, from first impression and opinion on to clarifying revelation! "Whether they were in the body or out of the body, they could not tell; for it did seem unto them like a transfiguration of them, that they were changed from this body of flesh into an immortal state, that they could behold the things of God." (3 Nephi 28:15.)

Next he wrote; "And now, whether they were mortal or immortal, from the day of their transfiguration, I know not." (3 Nephi 28:17.)

Subsequently, he received clarifying revelation and declared this; it's worth just a moment more: "But behold, since I wrote, I have inquired of the Lord, and he hath made it manifest unto me that there must needs be a change wrought upon their bodies, or else it needs be that they must taste of death; therefore, that they might not taste of death there was a change wrought upon their bodies, that they might not suffer pain nor sorrow save it were for the sins of the world.

"Now this change was not equal to that which shall take place at the last day; but there was a change wrought upon them, insomuch that Satan could have no power over them, that he could not tempt them; and they were sanctified in the flesh, that they were holy, and that the powers of the earth could not hold them. And in this state they were to remain until the judgment day of Christ; and at that day they were to receive a greater change, and to be received into the kingdom of the Father to go no more out, but to dwell with God eternally in the heavens." (3 Nephi 28:37-40.)

RACHEL: I'm going to add that episode to my "case studies." Thank you, Winston! Your son must be seriously studying the scriptures while on his mission.

WINSTON: He is, and I'm so pleased!

JEFFREY: Striking a balance between seeking and being content to wait for further light and knowledge would appear to be no small task!

NOEL: A balance, Jeffrey, between our readiness and the Lord's willingness. But a cascade can follow a pause as the Lord said: "If thou shalt ask, thou shalt receive revelation upon revelation, knowledge upon knowledge, that thou mayest know the mysteries and peaceable things—that which bringeth joy, that which bringeth life eternal." (D&C 42:61.)

JEFFREY: But before revelation, there is usually perspiration. So, genuine spirituality involves genuine struggle and searching, not just a passive repose or a leisurely waiting for information to be given.

CHARLES: However, there are real risks with revelation, especially if we are not meek, as we are cautioned in the Doctrine and Covenants. Where much is given, much is expected: "Although a man may have many revelations, and have power to do many mighty works, yet if he boasts in his own strength, and sets at naught the counsels of God, and follows after the dictates of his own will and carnal desires, he must fall and incur the vengeance of a just God upon him." (D&C 3:4.)

JEFFREY: A needed caveat, Charles! After all, the things to be searched most rigorously are, naturally, the holy scriptures.

CHARLES: The veritable treasure trove that so many disdain!

JEFFREY: A treasure trove, Charles, with which you are apparently becoming ever more familiar. Hear these words from Nephi and John: "And now I, Nephi, cannot say more; the Spirit stoppeth mine utterance, and I am left to mourn because of the unbelief, and the wickedness, and the ignorance, and the stiffneckedness of men; for they will not search knowledge, nor understand great knowledge, when it is given unto them in plainness, even as plain as word can be." (2 Nephi 32:7.)

"And now, whoso readeth, let him understand;
he that hath the scriptures, let him search them."
(3 Nephi 10:14.)

"Search the scriptures; for in them ye think ye have
eternal life: and they are they which testify of me."
(John 5:39.)

PAULINE: But with the searching there is also waiting.
It seems to me that spirituality also involves genuine
patience—as Noel once said, a willingness to wait for
what is metered out to us.

NOEL: And on occasion, Pauline, even a willingness
to accept deliberate divine withholding; this occurred
even during the visit of the resurrected Jesus to the
Nephites: "When they shall have received this, which
is expedient that they should have first, to try their
faith, and if it shall so be that they shall believe these
things then shall the greater things be made manifest
unto them. . . . Behold, I was about to write them, all
which were engraven upon the plates of Nephi, but
the Lord forbade it, saying: I will try the faith of my
people." (3 Nephi 26:9, 11.)

The Lord even declared that, in effect, He tutors us
as little children, balancing our capacities to receive
and our abilities to bear: "Behold, ye are little children
and ye cannot bear all things now; ye must grow in
grace and in the knowledge of the truth." (D&C 50:40.)

WINSTON: But isn't God careful not to add unduly to
our accountability—I mean beyond our readiness to
receive?

NOEL: Yes, and some parables played a part in that
pattern of merciful and metered disclosure.

PAULINE: In a discussion last week within Jeffrey's extended family, his brother commented on how gain-

ing spiritual knowledge also requires us to become accustomed to working with summational knowledge.

NOEL: You mean the headlines, distillations, and chief generalizations of the centuries?

PAULINE: Yes. Much as we might like more details, such could be diversions from the summations.

NOEL: What you say seems to be the case. If I can find the references . . . Yes, first from Third Nephi and then Jacob: "There cannot be written in this book even a hundredth part of the things which Jesus did truly teach unto the people." (3 Nephi 26:6.)

"If there were preaching which was sacred, or revelation which was great, or prophesying, that I should engraven the heads of them upon these plates, and touch upon them as much as it were possible, for Christ's sake, and for the sake of our people." (Jacob 1:4.)

But back to spiritual experiences. Even these are no substitute for intellectual effort. In fact, the Lord still wants us to comprehend and verify for ourselves the doctrines even though we have had spiritual experiences. It was so with both Paul and Alma. (Alma 5:46.) In any event, regarding obtaining spiritual knowledge, vista follows upon vista, divine disclosure upon divine disclosure, "precept upon precept, line upon line." (Isaiah 28:13.)

CHARLES: I'm especially glad to hear you say that, Noel. It has seemed to me that neither our love of the Lord nor our love of spiritual learning can be characterized by a single, brisk dash followed by repose. It seems to involve such a tireless search and such a continuous process!

NOEL: "Here a little, and there a little," said Isaiah. (Isaiah 28:10.)

RACHEL: How true! This is not a process for the impatient. Genuine doubters who want answers to their questions can find them. But lazy doubters seem almost to avoid genuine inquiry and the search of resolution. Like Amulek, they "would not know." (Alma 10:6.)

WINSTON: I take some succor, however, Rachel, from George MacDonald's assertion that sincere doubt can, finally, prove to be productive. Listen to this: "Doubt must precede every deeper assurance; for uncertainties are what we first see when we look into a region hitherto unknown, unexplored, unannexed."[1]

CHARLES: MacDonald was the mentor *in absentia* of C. S. Lewis. And how discerning; his words put Thomas's doubt into a somewhat different perspective.

WINSTON: But the stress should be, as Rachel said, upon honest doubt that seeks resolution. Some doubters, incredibly, move away from contact with the Book of Mormon in order to test it! What they need to do is to read, discuss, and share it. Some deliberately become less active in the Church by getting busy with substitutes, much as Amulek did. (Alma 10:4-6.) But it seems to me that isolation is a poor forum for such evaluation.

CHARLES: Indeed it is, Winston. As I've watched my few disaffiliating friends, some even experience a false freedom at first. Strange how some who exit like a lot of notoriety but others slip away quietly. Some suddenly take out spiritual bankruptcy to everyone's surprise. Other doubters are so obviously anxious to run with the herd. They act as if they hear a warning Klaxon, signaling a last chance for them to enter that "great and spacious building." (1 Nephi 8:1.) They act as if its doors were about to be closed for the last time, and they flee so quickly to be with the lonely crowd!

NOEL: It is surprising, isn't it, that some panic so easily? Or are so shallowly rooted that they are toppled so easily?

CHARLES: Worse still, Noel, one unrooted tree can topple other unrooted trees in the process.

NOEL: Impatience and superficiality just won't do, will they? Especially since spiritual learning sometimes requires us to wait for the readying and relevant personal experiences.

RACHEL: Which may even include tutoring reproof!

JEFFREY: Exactly, Rachel! In any event, overlying all of this is the matter of the Lord's timetable and also the need for us to develop our personal capacity to decide. Note what these revelations from the Doctrine and Covenants suggest: "And if this be the case, I command you, my servant Joseph, that you shall say unto him, that he shall do no more, nor trouble me any more concerning this matter." (D&C 5:29.)

"Behold, this is according to the law and the prophets; wherefore, trouble me no more concerning this matter." (D&C 59:22.)

"Joseph, my son, if thou livest until thou art eighty-five years old, thou shalt see the face of the Son of Man; therefore let this suffice, and trouble me no more on this matter." (D&C 130:15.)

WINSTON: Hmmm. Jeffrey, as I check them, the chronology of those sections is interesting. I suppose that is your point. The dates of those revelations (1829, 1831, and 1843) suggest that Joseph was still being tutored as to timing—even just a year before his martyr-dom!

CHARLES: Frankly, I hadn't noticed that before.

Earlier someone said that spiritual knowledge requires meekness. Meekness can protect us against prideful and wrong intent, can't it?

NOEL: It can and does! We must never discount the inclusiveness and perfectness of God's judgment, for He judges men according to their motives, the desires of their hearts. With His discernment, it is possible. However, mortal systems are usually too clumsy to discover intent. For instance, it is clear in our time that lust and greed, that ancient alliance, have re-formed and commercialized around pornography but try to clothe themselves in the first amendment to make it difficult to deal with them.

CHARLES: But, Noel, it is solely mortal standards with which mortal systems of justice are concerned.

NOEL: True, Charles, but you see my point. God's justice will be perfect precisely because He will judge not only conduct but intent. (See Jeremiah 17:10.) Not only our behavior but our intent, our comparative knowledge or ignorance concerning a particular standard.

In any event, as secularism—with increasing impatience—seeks to sweep everything before it, even more courage will be required to stand against the tide. Remember, Pilate found no fault with Jesus but still turned Him over to the mob, even when Pilate knew exactly what the mob would do. (Luke 23:13-25.)

CHARLES: You see modern equivalents of that crucifying mob, don't you, Noel?

NOEL: Yes, I do, and the more sophisticates in the

makeup of the "mob," the less likely they are to regard themselves as a "mob."

CHARLES: A hopeful note, however. Apparently some of those in Jerusalem's ecclesiastical elite who were secret believers in Jesus still courageously came around later. Thanks to the new publications of the scriptures, I spotted this cross reference: "The word of God increased; and the number of the disciples multiplied in Jerusalem greatly; and a great company of the priests were obedient to the faith." (Acts 6:7.) Not just a few, but a "great company" of priests!

RACHEL: Thank you for that, Charles! Now maybe I can get some sympathy for my view that the rich young man who went away sorrowing may have come back later on to accept Jesus' call!

CHARLES: Redemptive Rachel! Even when one is making some spiritual progress, by the way, and even when he is blessed with meekness and some spirituality, still he had better not draw hasty conclusions. My friend C. S. Lewis wrote that if a follower of Christ were stronger, such a one might "be less tenderly treated." If braver, he might be sent "with far less help, to defend far more desperate posts."[2]

NOEL: The Lord leads us along, and He alone can decide when we are ready and for what post in the great battle.

RACHEL: I'm excited but I'm also sobered by what has been said tonight. In spiritual learning, however, even though there is progress, with each step forward the pupil comes to have an even better view of the wide and deep chasm between him and Christ. But it is such a breathtaking chasm! Even for the faithful follower! One's own imperfections loom even larger.

NOEL: Hence Nephi's lamentation, Rachel: "Notwithstanding the great goodness of the Lord, in showing me his great and marvelous works, my heart exclaimeth: O wretched man that I am! Yea, my heart sorroweth because of my flesh; my soul grieveth because of mine iniquities." (2 Nephi 4:17.)

JEFFREY: Even when spiritual knowledge is attained by immense individual effort, God's gifts to us are still gifts. It was so with Solomon and his gift of wisdom: "God said unto him, Because thou hast asked this thing, and hast not asked for thyself, nor hast asked the life of thine enemies; but hast asked for thyself understanding to discern judgment; behold, I have done according to thy words: lo, I have given thee a wise and an understanding heart; so that there was none like thee before thee, neither after thee shall any arise like unto thee. (1 Kings 3:11, 12.)

"God gave Solomon wisdom and understanding exceeding much, and largeness of heart, even as the sand that is on the sea shore." (1 Kings 4:29.)

CHARLES: But Solomon's legendary wisdom was accredited, Jeffrey. Spiritual knowledge usually goes unaccredited and unrecognized by the world. In fact, it is often mocked, disdained, and despised or "set at naught."

JEFFREY: It may all reflect, Charles, the unbelievers' easy and customary stereotyping of spiritual individuals. One must finally deal with truths, however, not labels. Some Corinthians might have typed Paul as an eccentric tentmaker. But he was an apostle of the Lord Jesus Christ!

WINSTON: Yes. Other of the early Church leaders were labeled as members of the sect of the Nazarenes.

Some thought them to be seditious. (Acts 24:5.) Yet, Gamaliel seems to have had more perspective or tolerance. (Acts 5:34.)

CHARLES: My guess, by the way, is that Gamaliel's wisdom was not rooted in the notion of pluralism and tolerance. He was uneasy. He really wanted caution to be exercised by the Jewish leaders because the Christians might be right! Time—not labels—would tell, Gamaliel was saying.

NOEL: May we go back to Charles's point about how spiritual knowledge is unaccredited by some? Even what we do know spiritually is difficult to share, even "the smallest part," as Alma said: "Behold, who can glory too much in the Lord? Yea, who can say too much of his great power, and of his mercy, and of his long-suffering towards the children of men? Behold, I say unto you, I cannot say the smallest part which I feel." (Alma 26:16.)

PAULINE: Have we not all felt that same frustration in our attempts at articulation? Including with our children? We are even sharply warned by Jesus that some will disregard divine data. "Give not that which is holy unto the dogs, neither cast ye your pearls before swine, lest they trample them under their feet, and turn again and rend you." (Matthew 7:6.)

WINSTON: Hmmm. I noticed, Pauline, in the reading list you and Jeffrey gave us for tonight that the Joseph Smith Translation of that verse gives us both confirmation and elaboration. Listen to his rendition of that terse verse, that stern passage—it was scarcely a soothing "public relations" pronouncement: "The mysteries of the kingdom ye shall keep within yourselves; for it is not meet to give that which is holy unto the dogs; neither cast ye your pearls unto swine, lest they trample them under their feet. For the world cannot receive that which ye, yourselves, are not able to bear; wherefore ye shall not give your pearls unto them, lest they turn again and rend you." (Matthew 7:10, 11, JST.)

RACHEL: As usual, Brother Joseph helps us to understand better. In contrast to what Pauline rightly noted, what a rich experience it is, however, when two individuals can, unimpeded, share spiritual knowledge with the help of the Holy Ghost. Listen and enjoy: "I, Nephi, cannot write all the things which were taught among my people; neither am I mighty in writing, like unto speaking; for when a man speaketh by the power of the Holy Ghost the power of the Holy Ghost carrieth it unto the hearts of the children of men. (2 Nephi 33:1.)

"Why is it that ye cannot understand and know, that he that receiveth the word by the Spirit of truth receiveth it as it is preached by the Spirit of truth? wherefore, he that preacheth and he that receiveth, understand one another, and both are edified and rejoice together." (D&C 50:21, 22.)

NOEL: The true disciple knows that he knows. Furthermore, God knows that he knows. So spiritual knowledge, as Charles said earlier, is a weighty responsibility.

RACHEL: But when we rigorously study, fast, pray, and apply gospel principles, we can actually know of ourselves that something is true by the process of revelation. Recall Alma? (Alma 5:45-47.)

NOEL: In fact, no one, by himself and by thought processes alone, can really know the ways of the Lord.

God's thoughts and ways are so much higher than man's ways—unless such things are revealed by the Lord. (Isaiah 55:8-9.) Jacob said, "Behold, great and marvelous are the works of the Lord. How unsearchable are the depths of the mysteries of him; and it is impossible that man should find out all his ways. And no man knoweth of his ways save it be revealed unto him; wherefore, brethren, despise not the revelations of God." (Jacob 4:8.)

Moreover, the broadened and deepened disclosure by the Spirit of "things as they really are" (Jacob 4:13) includes not only the truths of the universe's grand realities but also truths about our own inadequacies. This, too, is part of the revealing role of the Holy Ghost. Jacob wrote, "The Lord God showeth us our weakness that we may know that it is by his grace, and his great condescensions unto the children of men, that we have power to do these things." (Jacob 4:7.)

When we acquire this knowledge, though, it is not obtained temporally, but spiritually, as Alma asserted: "I would not that ye think that I know of myself—not of the temporal but of the spiritual, not of the carnal mind but of God." (Alma 36:4.)

The Holy Ghost knows all things as a member of the Godhead. If we will let Him, He can reveal all necessary things to us. The Lord said, "It shall be given by the Comforter, the Holy Ghost, that knoweth all things." (D&C 35:19.)

JEFFREY: Paul's words about how the Spirit of God searcheth "the deep things" match Jacob's, don't they? About how the Spirit teaches us of "things as they really are"? (1 Corinthians 2:10, 11; Jacob 4:13.)

CHARLES: They surely do, Jeffrey. There is almost

constant correlation. But, I say again, such revelatory abundance can bring anxieties and responsibilities. This verse was also on tonight's reading list: "Behold, you should not have feared man more than God. Although men set at naught the counsels of God, and despise his words." (D&C 3:7.) We can receive God's counsel and set it "at naught" and then be in worse shape than before.

NOEL: No wonder we mortals are counseled by Jacob not to despise the revelations of God! (Jacob 4:8.)

JEFFREY: These revelations, however, are actually the doorway to a whole realm of knowledge, a realm that will otherwise go undiscovered. This is the central point Pauline and I want to make tonight.

PAULINE: But even so, these things of great worth are often trampled under some mortals' feet as things of naught. "But behold, there are many that harden their hearts against the Holy Spirit, that it hath no place in them; wherefore, they cast many things away which are written and esteem them as things of naught." (2 Nephi 33:2.) Some truly do regard spiritual things as "naught," as having the significance of a cipher, or as being nonexistent.

WINSTON: But the adventure of seeking spiritual knowledge is so much worth it. These last few months have been so special for me—the joys of having a son on a mission . . . this group . . . well, you understand my feelings, I hope.

    If it's time, Jeffrey and Pauline, for sharing, I brought along what President Brigham Young said about the role of individual experience and capacity in the mortal process: "We are here to get an experience, and we cannot increase in that any faster than our capacities will admit. Our capacities are limited, though sometimes we could receive more than we do, but we will not. . . .

"Take the history of this Church from the commencement, and we have proven that we cannot receive all the Lord has for us. We have proven to the heavens and to one another that we are not yet capacitated to receive all the Lord has for us, and that we have not yet a disposition to receive all he has for us. Can you understand that there is a time you can receive and there is a time you cannot receive, a time when there is no place in the heart to receive? The heart of man will be closed up, the will will be set against this and that that we have opportunity to receive. There is an abundance the Lord has for the people, if they would receive it."[3]

"When we consider the immensity of knowledge and wisdom and understanding pertaining to the things of this life, pertaining to the learning of this world, pertaining to that which is within our reach, and ready for the use and profit of the people, and particularly with regard to taking care of ourselves, and then consider our shortcomings, and slothfulness, we may look upon ourselves with shamefacedness because of the smallness of our attainments in the midst of so many great advantages."[4]

CHARLES: "Shamefacedness because of the smallness of our attainments." Very good! Since we are now pooling what we brought to share, I was struck by these statements, also from Brigham Young. These concern divine tutoring amid trials: "Place a man in a situation where he is obliged or compelled, in order to sustain himself, to have faith in the name of Jesus Christ, and it brings him to a point where he will know for himself; and happy are those who pass through trials, if they maintain their integrity and their faith to their calling."[5]

RACHEL: No wonder, then, there is such divine determination at times.

CHARLES: Yes. This next quotation, also from Brigham Young, reminds me of me, at least sometimes: "There are some who are always fearful, trembling, doubting, wavering, and at the same time doing everything they can for the promotion of righteousness. Yet they are in doubts whether they are doing the best possible good, and they fear and fail here and there, and will doubt their own experience and the witness of the Spirit to them."[6]

WINSTON: It's interesting to see the correlation in our individual preparation. I've another from President Young: "The expression, *"true believer,"* needs qualifying, for many believe *who do not obey*—I will qualify it by saying, a believer in Jesus Christ, who manifests his faith to God, angels, and his brethren, by his obedience. Not but that there are believers who do not obey, but the only true believers are they who *prove their belief* by their obedience to the requirements of the Gospel."[7]

In fact, President Young even referenced the seeming lack of intellectual integrity; he described the intellectual "infidelity" of disbelievers in the face of so much data: "The infidel looks abroad and sees the works of nature, in all their diversity—the mountain piercing the clouds with its snowy peaks, the mighty river, fertilizing, in its course to the sea, the valleys and plains in every direction, the sun in his glory at mid-day, the moon in her silvery splendor, and the myriad organizations from man to the minutest form of insect life, all giving the most irrefutable evidence of a designer and creator of infinite wisdom, skill and power, and yet he says there is no Deity, no Supreme Ruler, but all is the result of blind chance. How preposterous! Now, here is a book called the Bible. It is enclosed in what we call the cover, consisting of boards, paper and leather. Within the covers we see a vast amount of writing—syllables, words and sentences; now if we say there never was a person to compose, write, print or bind this book, but that it is here wholly as the result of chance, we shall only give expression to the faith, if faith it can be called, of those who are termed infidels; in fact this is infidelity."[8]

JEFFREY: Choice quotations! Thanks to all for your usual stimulating participation and careful preparation. Time for our prayer and refreshments.

RACHEL: But we have been fed so well spiritually . . .

CHARLES: Before we conclude, is there not an intrinsic spiritual resonance in some individuals that facilitates this whole process?

NOEL: A perceptive question, and the answer is yes. Your question gives me a chance to use these special lines I brought along from Joseph Smith about such resonance: "Every word that proceedeth from the mouth of Jehovah has such an influence over the human mind—the logical mind—that it is convincing without other testimony; faith comes by hearing."[9]

CHARLES: Thanks for that, Noel. Finally, if Pauline does not mind waiting a moment, I thought, at long last, that we were promised a few words on petitionary prayer?

JEFFREY: Yes, that promise was made. Noel has that assignment.

NOEL: All right. Let us examine, but only briefly, as the hour is so late, petitionary prayer. If every prayer were always answered with the results requested, either we would be omniscient mortals who never ask amiss, or we would be dealing with a powerful but permissive god.

Since it is also clear that we can, on occasion, ask amiss, we need to be concerned with that possibility. (2 Nephi 4:35; see also James 4:3.) As we think about prayer, certain things become abundantly evident. Sometimes we simply fail to ask. Many times we may lack the faith in a certain thing to back our particularized petitions.

CHARLES: We are told, however, that if we ask, we shall receive. Listen to this: "All things, whatsoever ye shall ask in prayer, believing, ye shall receive." (Matthew 21:22.)

NOEL: But we often press our petitions on the Lord out of our limited perspective of three words in this declaration by the resurrected Jesus: "Whatsoever ye shall ask the Father in my name, *which is right*, believing that ye shall receive, behold it shall be given unto you." (3 Nephi 18:20, italics added.) However, when our very prayers are inspired, then they are granted. A group of ancient Americans got specific guidance . . . here it is: "For it was given unto them what they should pray." (3 Nephi 19:24.) So, as noted in Matthew and confirmed through Joseph Smith, "he that asketh in the Spirit asketh according to the will of God; wherefore it is done even as he asketh. (D&C 46:30; see also Helaman 10:5.)

PAULINE: Don't we also need to take account of the free agency of others? They, too, are part of the equation of our petition.

NOEL: So true, Pauline. Even when what we request is asked for in faith and would also be right, there is the matter of the agency of others and also the matter of God's timing, which we discussed earlier.

JEFFREY: Sometimes, too, we ask, but lazily—having, like Oliver Cowdery, taken no thought save it were to ask. (D&C 9:7.)

NOEL: If pressed, I would say that such effortless prayer is faithless prayer, just as that scripture indicates, Jeffrey.

CHARLES: Noel, I like your comments that imply the interplay of God's omniscience and man's agency. Such an understanding will preserve us from the cruelty of this dilemma as put by C. S. Lewis: "If God were good, He would wish to make His creatures perfectly happy, and if God were almighty He would be able to do what he wished. But the creatures are not happy. Therefore God lacks either goodness, or power, or both."[10]

The answer is, of course, that God's plan is to develop us, not just to see that we have a good time. This objective is at the center of it all. Lewis again: "To ask that God's love should be content with us as we are is to ask that God should cease to be God. . . . Because He already loves us He must labour to make us lovable."[11]

Against that backdrop, here are Lewis's wise words about petitionary prayer: "We can bear to be refused, but not to be ignored. In other words, our faith can survive many refusals if they are refusals, and not mere disregards."[12]

PAULINE: I so agree, Charles. Whenever we ask amiss, because God loves us as a loving and perfect Father, He cannot grant our petition. (See 3 Nephi 18:20; D&C 46:30.)

RACHEL: No wonder the Lord urges us on, sometimes so relentlessly, in the journey of life. We live within range of striking distance of such immense possibilities; the tiny mustard seed is actually but a faint foreshadowing.

CHARLES: Yes! Meanwhile, however, our idleness as to spiritual things can caress our carnal appetites just as doubt can depress and dampen our faith. It seems to matter little to the adversary whether we become sensual or casual; either way, we are lost to things of the Spirit.

WINSTON: Well said, Charles. Furthermore, if people cease believing in a loving God, who is also omnicompetent, they will not likely take their problems to Him.

*(Not more than half an hour later, the group departs into a night of falling snow. For a brief moment, Charles and Winston pause at curbside and speak together, almost reverently.)*

CHARLES: The moonlight makes the falling snow seem like flakes of fire, Winston, a perfect match for the burning in my bosom!

# Seventh Conversation: Cares of the World

"The cares of this world, and the deceitfulness of
riches, and the lusts of other things entering in,
choke the word, and it becometh unfruitful."
(Mark 4:19.)

*The setting: A late spring evening on the veranda of
Charles's home. All are present. For the first time, Charles is
leading a discussion. The discussion concerns the constant
challenge of not being too caught up in the cares of the world,
the stress that accompanies being in the world without becoming of the world. The discussion is in progress.*

---

NOEL: As you just said, Charles, it is so easy, if one is
not careful, to pass over the deeply significant words
of Jesus. They are so densely packed with divine counsel and reflect His centuries of Saviorhood.

CHARLES: His directions are relevance itself! Among his words are those with which He warns us, very directly, about not becoming entangled in the "cares of the world." (Mark 4:19; Luke 8:14; 21:34.)

WINSTON: Interesting, isn't it, how on the surface worldly cares would seem to be a mere minor distraction with which everyone ought to be able to cope? Yet so often the spiritual things instead come to be regarded as the distraction, a subtle but awful reversal of priorities.

CHARLES: Yes, and I find too that even a touching, spiritual moment can be so quickly lost in the bustle of an afternoon's traffic jam, in the cares of tonight's phone calls, or because of the pressures brought by tomorrow's mail or preparation for a meeting of the faculty council.

PAULINE: I agree! The world "is too much with us."

RACHEL: Sometimes the cares of the moment seem to hover over us like a dark cloud cover, causing us to see reality less clearly. The anxiety of the moment, such as worrying over one's health, can be allowed to dominate everything else.

CHARLES: This, of course, is why we all need the bracing sea breeze of the scriptures to blow those cloud covers away. Then, to quote Jacob, we can see things "as they really are." (Jacob 4:13.) Oh, how I am coming to love Jacob the poet-prophet.

RACHEL: But our cares and concerns are real; it's simply that they are not the whole of reality.

WINSTON: Exactly why perspective is so vital, Rachel. For instance, Jesus noted how the "children of this world"—because of the intensity of their dedication to their secular objectives—are anxiously looking and planning ahead, coming to terms with the world *as they see it*. Hence they are, in one sense, "wiser than the children of light" or Church members. (Luke 16:8.)

PAULINE: How true! The "children of this world" are, in fact, often more "anxiously engaged" in their causes than some of us are in God's cause. (See D&C 58:27.) We are so slow in truly coming to terms with "things as they really are."

CHARLES: I've often wondered if those stark warnings from Jesus about the cares of the world were not given especially to the slack servant, the developing disciple—one, for instance, who may still listen with too eager an ear for the praise of the world.

JEFFREY: Or, likewise, to one who, in his quest for belonging, still yearns overmuch for a place in the secular synagogue. (John 12:42, 43.)

WINSTON: Also, how acquisitive we are! Constantly striving to add just one more creature comfort, which will, ere long, moulder anyway, and meanwhile neglecting the entreaties of the Creator of the world, Who has, after all, promised to give the faithful everything He has! (D&C 84:38.)

JEFFREY: No vocational pun intended, but the scriptures give us excellent investment counseling concerning preparing for the riches of eternity. It is available! But it is not forced upon us.

CHARLES: How, therefore, can one better manage these cares or "anxieties" of the world? This is our focus tonight.

We live on this earth. We must breathe its air, drink

its water, and use its fuel, shelter, and food. Clearly, we are not yet to take leave of this world. Moreover, since we must experience the sweat of the brow by working usefully in the world, our work should not be performed indifferently.

RACHEL: Furthermore, we should be genuinely appreciative of all those believers, unbelievers, and disbelievers alike—who do well the necessary and useful work of the world, such as gifted doctors.

CHARLES: Yes! An agnostic can make a significant scientific discovery to better the health of mankind. A misbehaving individual can produce some brilliant music or poetry, though not as good as he might have done if he had been pure. (See D&C 133:45.) A generous God accredits all such human goodness, recognizing it even from those who will not recognize Him.

NOEL: I lament, however, that so much mortal genius is given over to eloquent descriptions of human misery, and especially the implication that such misery is inevitable and unavoidable! You've made your case, though, Charles, that disengaging from the cares of the world does not mean withdrawal from the world. In fact, Jesus' followers are told to be a leaven or a salt among the people of the world by being *in* the world but not *of* it: "I pray not that thou shouldest take them out of the world, but that thou shouldest keep them from the evil." (John 17:15.)

PAULINE: I so agree! Forsaking the world does not mean monasticism or asceticism either. Instead, it requires equipoise, spiritual balance, lest one "gain the whole world, and lose his own soul." (Matthew 16:26.)

JEFFREY: Paul sensibly prescribed setting our affection upon "things above, not on things on the earth." (Colossians 3:2.) Why? Because such gross unhappiness can be caused by prosperity without a purpose. As Samuel the Lamanite observed, poor perspective impoverishes even a rich people who "do not remember the Lord your God in the things with which he hath blessed you, but ye do always remember your riches, not to thank the Lord your God for them; yea, your hearts are not drawn out unto the Lord, but they do swell with great pride, unto boasting, and unto great swelling, envyings, strifes, malice, persecutions, and murders, and all manner of iniquities." (Helaman 13:22; see also Helaman 7:21.)

PAULINE: No wonder we are warned specifically against getting our hearts set so much upon the things of the world. (D&C 121:35.) Instead, we are to set our first priorities on building up the kingdom of God. (See Matthew 6:33, JST.)

CHARLES: You have all created a convincing montage by your commentary. The challenge is as subtle as it is real. Even the unavoidable cares of the world can consume us. Routineness and busyness, in and of themselves, are not bad, but their steady drumbeat can distract us. Besides, busyness is no substitute for purpose and meaning.

RACHEL: In fact, Charles, such preoccupation also causes us to commit sins of omission.

NOEL: Was this not part of the challenge of our much-discussed rich and righteous young man who knelt at Jesus' feet in sincere inquiry? (Mark 10:17-22.) He lacked one thing—the submissiveness to do as bidden: give his goods to the poor, take up the cross, and follow Jesus. He was actually called by Christ but not chosen! Why? Because his heart was so set upon the things of this world. (D&C 121:35.)

JEFFREY: In contrast, Noel, that remarkable man Moses determined to forego being called "the son of Pharaoh's daughter." Why? Because Moses esteemed "the reproach of Christ greater riches than the treasures in Egypt." (Hebrews 11:24, 26.) Moses chose Christ and affliction with the people of God rather than ease among the elite Egyptians!

NOEL: By the way, the very law of Moses, as Jacob declared, was designed for "pointing our souls" to Him, to Jesus of Nazareth. (Jacob 4:5.)

CHARLES: A few steps back, please. The tragedy of the rich, young, commandment-keeping man who ran to Jesus and knelt at His feet was not that he dishonestly acquired or misused his wealth, but that he was underusing his life! He neglected the real purposes of life. The beckoning call came to him from Jesus to use his ample goodness and talent to greater effect. It was declined. The young man was diverted; the cares of the world, once again, usurped the place of more important things.

NOEL: Rachel, in her empathy, continues to insist, Charles, that perhaps that young man later came back to Jesus to say he'd changed his mind.

RACHEL: Remember the prodigal!

JEFFREY: How can we forget him? One can be consumed by the legitimate cares of the world, as in the case of this young man. A willingness, therefore, to subordinate ourselves to further spiritual discipline from the Lord is the key to real spiritual triumph.

NOEL: It seems to me that next to direction, balance is often the key to walking the strait and narrow path. This path is certainly not located at the bottom of a ravine into which all slide naturally and inexorably. It is just the opposite; the strait and narrow path is on a ridge with deep ravines on each side.

WINSTON: So true, Noel. In balancing the cares of the world we, for instance, must strive for economic adequacy and to provide for our own families. There is nothing wrong either with placing sufficient in store so that the needs of the morrow can be cared for. At the same time, however, it is so easy to become, if not obsessed, at least too preoccupied by the things of this world.

NOEL: Similarly, there is nothing wrong with receiving sincere commendations, *unless* the praise of the world turns our heads and becomes something about which we come to care too much or that would distort our decision making.

CHARLES: Agreed. As I prepared for this evening, it amazed me how scriptural history gives us stern warnings. It is difficult for the Lord's people, even when they reach prosperity through obedience and righteousness, to be able to sustain those same conditions without lapsing back into patterns of unrighteousness. The maxim about not being able to "stand a little prosperity" appears to be soberingly accurate. We are so quick to forget our God. Listen, please, to these words from Helaman: "At the very time when [the Lord] doth prosper his people, yea, in the increase of their fields, their flocks and their herds, and in gold, and in silver, and in all manner of precious things of every kind and art; sparing their lives, and delivering them out of the hands of their enemies; softening the hearts of their enemies that they should not declare wars against them; yea, and in fine, doing all things for the welfare and happiness of his people; yea, then is the time that they do harden their hearts, and do forget the Lord their God, and do trample under their feet the Holy One—yea, and this because of their ease, and their exceedingly great prosperity.

"And thus we see that except the Lord doth chasten his people with many afflictions, yea, except he doth visit them with death and with terror, and with famine and with all manner of pestilence, they will not remember him." (Helaman 12:2, 3.)

WINSTON: Hmmm. Given those general warnings, but in such specific forms, think what a challenge it is to be meek and nonacquisitive. Apparently our souls are genuinely at risk, but especially so in the presence of power, riches, and idleness.

JEFFREY: Idleness is risky! Though we crave it and sometimes confuse it with leisure, idleness is different from the serenity of the soul brought by the promised peace of the Spirit. (John 14:27.) Here's something from Nephi and from the Doctrine and Covenants: "Because of their cursing which was upon them they did become an idle people, full of mischief and subtlety, and did seek in the wilderness for beasts of prey." (2 Nephi 5:24.)

"Behold, they have been sent to preach my gospel among the congregations of the wicked; wherefore, I give unto them a commandment, thus: Thou shalt not idle away thy time, neither shalt thou bury thy talent that it may not be known." (D&C 60:13.)

RACHEL: Are we saying, then, that turbulence and dissonance in our lives have their uses? Is there no other way? Why can't we be sufficiently humble "because of the word" instead of depending so much upon vexing circumstances? (See Alma 32:16.)

NOEL: No one, Rachel, wishes more than the Lord that we would be humble "because of the word."

CHARLES: In such stress and dissonance, our perceptivity will actually depend on our humility. Failure to see that which is ominously developing below the surface is so common because of the heavy preoccupation with the things and cares of the moment.

WINSTON: This is a failure, Charles, not only of governments, so much of which I have witnessed during my career, but also of individuals. By the time the consequences of such insensitive heedlessness are seen, it is often too late!

NOEL: I think it happens because we can scarcely expect to see the full significance of trends and developments in the world if we are too much a part of the things of the world. Noah's contemporaries were much too busy, too preoccupied, with the cares of the world. It was life and business as usual.

PAULINE: By the way, the cares of the world, in one translation, are rendered as the *anxieties* of the world, the things over which many in the world worry, fret, and stew. These anxieties often involve real dangers, but even so, can obscure other real dangers.

NOEL: I'd not noticed that different rendering of "cares," Pauline. It broadens our focus, doesn't it? The very routineness of the cares of the world and the duties of the world can numb us, particularly when combined with the desensitizing that goes with sin!

PAULINE: In fact, Noel, it is directly because of iniquity, said Jesus, that the love of many will wax cold in the last days. (Matthew 24:12.)

CHARLES: Yes, Pauline! Is it not also true that one dimension of pride that manifests itself so stubbornly is found in those situations in which people choose the right, but, instead of putting their hand to the plow without looking back, they look back? Either they wish they could remake an earlier decision, or they want to possess the things of the world and at the same time possess the things of heaven.

NOEL: So true! Laman and Lemuel, like Lot's wife, looked back over their shoulder at Jerusalem, regretting the decision to leave—doubting the prophesied and impending fall of such a strong and seemingly invincible city.

CHARLES: Jerusalem's citizens were just as smug as the passengers on the Titanic! Ponder the even earlier ingratitude of the complaining children of Israel. At one point in the wilderness, they even complained that they were bereft of some of the comforts they had known while in bondage in Egypt. (Exodus 16:3.)

WINSTON: How lamentably true, Charles! Another dimension of pride—which can compound the cares of the world—is to be found in the way in which trivial matters are allowed to escalate far out of proportion to their importance. Whatever happened to those strippings from the cow that helped to trigger the prideful departure of Thomas B. Marsh from the Church? Where are those synagogues, now, in which sat some who secretly believed in Christ and in which they were so anxious not to lose their place?

JEFFREY: Those are powerful questions, Winston! To attempt to add to them: We read what a guilty Judas finally did with his thirty pieces of silver (Matthew 27:5-9.), but what finally happened to the estate of the rich and righteous young man who lacked one thing? (Luke 18:18-23.)

CHARLES: Our conversational "pile-ons" are getting better and better! Compared to our stretching premortal existence and the endless immortality to follow, this brief moment on this planet is of such fleeting duration. Besides, so much of what is acquired here cannot be taken on our journey home anyway.

RACHEL: In fact, Charles, most of the things on which we have spent our time, treasure, and talent are either inadmissible in the next world or will be obsolete.

WINSTON: Once again, like Lehi departing into the desert, it may be said of each of us, he "took nothing with him, save it were his family." (1 Nephi 2:4.)

PAULINE: And, don't forget, we will also take whatever degree of intelligence and spiritual attributes we acquired or further developed here. (D&C 130:18, 19.)

CHARLES: A very important reminder, Pauline. I wonder if, in seeking for spiritual poise in the midst of all these cares, the worldliness to be avoided is usually found to be more a matter of our personal traits than of our individual and formal roles. What do you think?

RACHEL: It seems so to me, Charles. The test is, are we, in developing our characters, drawing closer to the Lord or moving away from Him?

NOEL: The tug-of-war is constantly underway, Charles, in one degree or another, in almost every life. And tugs-of-war always involve stress and tension. Illustratively, we are to develop meekness (Moroni 7:44), but the pull of the world is all in the direction of pride.

CHARLES: Precisely. Pride prevents our serving with an eye *single* to the glory of God! I've even whimsically wondered about wearing an eye patch as a reminding symbol! We are to spend our lives in the service of others, but the world encourages selfishness, though it is often masked as authentic and impressive individualism.

NOEL: Further, Charles, we are to develop our capacity to love, on which so much else depends (Matthew 22:37-40), yet the world instead encourages lust. We are to develop our capacity for self-control, but the world pushes us in a direction of anger.

PAULINE: I so agree. And anger has rightly been described as "hell's furnace." (See Matthew 5:22.)

CHARLES: The gospel speaks of sharing and even consecration. The world emphasizes acquisition, even avarice: "Getting and spending we lay waste our mortal lives."

PAULINE: The gospel encourages us instead to emulate the characteristics of the Father and the Son. (Matthew 5:48; 3 Nephi 12:48; 27:27.) The gadarene impulse in the world, however, moves us ever in the direction of the herd.

WINSTON: Or, to mix metaphors, to join the march of the lemmings to the secular sea. Either way, it is the wrong kind of togetherness.

CHARLES: No wonder then, given the constant pull of the world, that Jesus said we are to deny ourselves *daily* and take up the cross *daily*, a continuous process rather than a single, dramatic act. (Luke 9:23.)

WINSTON: I'm impressed with how so much of spiritual maturity, therefore, consists of learning both *what* to love and *how* to love. If we are not careful, we will select the wrong objects or express defective love. Also, I'm impressed with how being more separated from the cares of the world can give place for us to care more for other people. (See Alma 5:57.)

RACHEL: Yes, Winston, given the incessant tug and pull of the world, no wonder we are given the counsel not to be "weary in well-doing." (Galatians 6:9; D&C 64:33.) This divine encouragement is given to keep us moving forward, carrying our crosses daily. Noel and I were discussing this very point with our married children last week. Young, dedicated couples can in their conscientiousness become truly weary, especially physically.

NOEL: The divine encouragement to persist may have also been given for yet another reason: to give us patience amid the seeming and real injustices and incongruities in the world. The psalmist speaks of the "ungodly, who prosper in the world." (Psalm 73:12.)

One translation of the words of the complaining and fainthearted in Malachi reads, "It is useless to serve God . . . what gain is it to do his bidding. . . . It is the worldly, we find, who are well off; evildoers prosper, they dare God—and they escape"! (Malachi 3:13, 14, Moffatt Version.)

RACHEL: Yet the promise-laden scriptures do tell us that we will be blessed according to our obedience to those laws upon which the blessings are predicated. (D&C 130:21.) If we keep the Lord's commandments, "he doth immediately bless" us. (Mosiah 2:24.)

JEFFREY: But, Rachel, faithful men and women are not always rewarded with blessings after the manner of the world, since we are to "forsake the world." (D&C 53:2.) We are already in such real danger of our hearts getting set "so much upon the things of this world" that we may fail to learn the great and essential lessons. (See D&C 121:35, 36.)

NOEL: True, Jeffrey, an excellent point! Hence, God will not bless us in ways that will interfere with our individual developmental needs. When meek Moses needed training on how to delegate, the Lord did not have him instructed on how to project his image as an omnicompetent leader. (See Exodus 18:17, 18.)

CHARLES: Once again, lest the point be lost, it is important to care about keeping intact this planet and living conditions on it. After all, it is the setting for our schooling in this probationary second estate. We do need food and water and shelter and adequate arrangements of all kinds. Thus certain of the work of the world is obviously necessary and useful. We must not, for instance, burn down the school in nuclear anger, either.

WINSTON: Hmmm. Yet the place is not the process, is it? The schoolhouse needs to be kept in good working order, but it is not the same thing as the teaching and learning that happen inside.

PAULINE: Agreed! Like a devoted custodian, some get entirely taken up with the schoolhouse. But you're right, Winston, the site is not the substance.

NOEL: Besides, too much anxiety over the things of this world indicates a lack of trust in God's foreknowledge. Our Schoolmaster apparently prefers that we live in "cheerful insecurity."

CHARLES: Apparently, if one can but accept the basic reality about this planet and God's use of it for His eternal purposes, then the things of the world take on quite a different meaning. The work of the world is necessary but ancillary to higher purposes.

JEFFREY: Even those particular clinical experiences through which we pass, the individualized courses of study, are part of a divine developmental design that, for now, we see through the "glass darkly." Later on, we shall see, clearly, the interplay of present deficiencies and future opportunities—and the "why" of certain of our intense learning experiences.

NOEL: True. Someday we will be able to view those clinical experiences with precious perspective. One's act of forgiveness in the midst of anguishing circumstances will later be seen as that which really mattered. The circumstances will have long since disappeared. Yet, at the time of trial, it was precisely those circumstances of that moment that were so preoccupying. The lesson in forgiveness may have seemed almost secondary. Later, just the opposite perspective will be ours.

CHARLES: In view of all these things, why is it, then, that we lose, or nearly lose, our perspective because of the cares of the world?

NOEL: For one thing, because this mortal experience has been so carefully designed. We truly feel it! It could not be otherwise. Often it is so close a passage that our full attention is needed. We cannot pass through it with just one hand upon the wheel while musing distractedly or philosophically over what is underway.

WINSTON: Furthermore, what is happening is happening to *us*, not to someone else. Clinical detachment is almost impossible! Anything less would mean that life's curriculum would have been too loosely designed and the learning too superficial!

NOEL: The Master Himself cried out on the cross, "I thirst." (John 19:28.) In deepest agony, Jesus expressed a very real, but passing, need. He did not issue a detached and relaxed communiqué on how far along, percentage-wise, the process of the atonement then was. He thirsted! Finally, another pending prophecy—about the cruel giving of vinegar instead of water—was fulfilled! (See Psalm 69:21.) Then came the three words, "It is finished." (John 19:30.)

WINSTON: On our scale, it is the same. We feel the heat of the refining fire, but the heat is not the product itself!

RACHEL: Likewise, Winston, our mortal schooling is not "finished" either—until the concluding bell rings!

CHARLES: It is precisely in such settings that we especially need the Lord "every hour"—and also families, friends, leaders, and neighbors—to help us maintain our spiritual composure and perspective.

May I take this opportunity to say how much you, my friends, mean to me? Particularly during the last two years as I've come to have a clearer perception of reality.

NOEL: We all feel, Charles, that our friendships are deepening as our discipleship deepens. We thank you, too.

PAULINE: How precious is the perspective of the gospel that permits us to see "things as they really are" and also "as they really will be." (Jacob 4:13.) By the way, only twice in all of scripture does this adverb *really* occur. Both times are in this one verse in Jacob! It is no accident!

JEFFREY: How perceptive!

RACHEL: I'd like to ask, if I may, about the matter of our agency and God's foreknowledge. Do any of you wish to venture forth on that one?

WINSTON: Hmmm! First to strike my mind is this thought: Imagine the delicacy . . . the precise ways in which God must communicate certain matters to us . . . in order to give us adequate but not overmuch help in making our way through this mortal estate. Yet not so much help that we would set at naught the developmental role of faith in this probationary and tutoring period.

NOEL: Hence, God can give certain knowledge only to the most trusted and spiritually mature of mortals.

RACHEL: Yet so many of us wish, sometimes desperately, to know what tomorrow or next year will bring. Or how long we will live. Or when the school bell will ring for oneself.

CHARLES: Why, then, the divine restraint as to disclosure?

NOEL: Because knowledge of certain *future* things could affect the way in which we use our agency *now*. Thus, the future would overhang and impose itself unduly upon the present. This would be counterproductive so far as the developmental purposes of the plan of salvation are concerned.

PAULINE: Also, because, by way of example, if someone knew "now" that he or she was, for instance, to have special status in the future, it would be tantamount to giving that person power in advance, especially if the knowledge became more widespread.

WINSTON: Hmmm. Very good! So far as the reaction of others to him or to her is concerned, there could be intimidation by anticipation. Such could crimp and constrain others as to how they respond to such a person in anticipation of the status to come. Agency and accountability would be so confused.

JEFFREY: Foreknowledge, if thus given unselectively and without divine guidance, would change "today" into "tomorrow." Instead, life is to be metered out to us daily.

RACHEL: Yes, Jeffrey, and sufficient unto each day, or period, or season of life, are the choices and challenges thereof. Frankly, these are sometimes "enough and to spare."

WINSTON: No wonder such foreknowledge is given sparingly, and then only to those least likely to abuse it. Otherwise we would always be living and deciding in advance, which would not be good.

NOEL: Sometimes even those to whom such foreknowledge is given by way of revelation or inspiration must hold it within themselves. Wonderingly or trustingly or both—such as Mary did, keeping certain things in her heart and pondering them. (Luke 2:19.)

Sometimes, too, the spiritually privileged are directed to withhold. Not only is it a matter of confidentiality but also of respect for the Lord's timing and a matter of deference to the agency of others, too.

JEFFREY: We are given enough, though, but not too much; more than we can manage, at times, by way of truth. But not so much as to be overwhelmed by it.

CHARLES: This extended sortie has been interesting. However, if you will forgive the pun, we'd better get back to the cares of the world . . .

WINSTON: As I struggle with the cares of the world, more and more it seems, as Noel observed, that the strait and narrow path is not a path located at the bottom of a steep ravine into which all mortals slide inevitably and relentlessly. In fact, if I may risk adding to Noel's analogy, it is just the other way around! The strait and narrow path is situated as if on a rising razorback, a steep, narrow path on each side of which are steep ravines. The path is not only steep and narrow but rock strewn; it can be navigated at times only when one is upon his hands and knees!

CHARLES: The very perils of moving along this path require such concentration! If the path were wide and not risk filled and all we had to do was to amble or drift, it would be so much easier. But there would be no meaningful individual responsibility, no decisions needed, except one: To stay close to the herd.

RACHEL: *(Almost to herself)* Adversity surely keeps the heart pounding rapidly. There is a certain tingling in the mind as we seek to advance on that challenging, stretching path that lies before us.

NOEL: *(With anxious glance at Rachel)* Yes. The adrenalin of adversity concentrates the mind wonderfully, doesn't it? It certainly rivets our attention on the things to be endured, to be decided, and to be understood. It should not surprise us, therefore, that one of the continually challenging requirements of walking the strait and narrow path is to keep our balance—meaning balance and poise in so many different ways.

WINSTON: It seems we must ever be watchful. The tilt and veer of the natural man is to one side or the other of the strait and narrow path.

CHARLES: I need, for instance, to develop humility and meekness, but the tendency of us mortals is toward pride. We are to develop patience, but the natural man is impatient. We are to be pure, but the natural man tends toward corruption. We are to be spiritually submissive, but the natural man tends toward selfishness and aggressiveness. We are to endure well, but, left to our natural tendencies, we would give up.

We are to be loving in order to be like Jesus, not hating, despising, or ignoring of others. We are to be hopeful, not despairing. We are to be kind, not selfish or inconsiderate.

JEFFREY: Exactly. Every day and every moment, the chance to slip is there, whether by slipping into rudeness in our conversation, or in a failure to listen, or in a burst of pride that can trample, intimidate, or, at least, disappoint others. How vital Christ is as our exemplar, our model! How vital He is as our Perfect Shepherd to lead us along in the strait and narrow path.

CHARLES: Well spoken, Jeffrey. Let's go back to that scripture that says the Lord will try the faith and the patience of His people. (Mosiah 23:21.) Presumably, my friends, that means trying our faith with regard to fundamentals, not peripheral issues, don't you think? In other words, as we have been saying, the fundamentals of faith involve faith in the Lord Jesus Christ and in our Heavenly Father's plan of salvation.

RACHEL: And in Joseph Smith. It seems critics are so quick to seize upon any minor imperfections in Joseph. Or any indications that, in his humanness, he reflected the environment in which he lived.

I brought along these lines from him, spoken from the temple stand in Nauvoo the month before his martyrdom: "I never told you I was perfect—but there is no error in the revelations which I have taught."[1]

And what flow came through him! In April, 1843, from that same stand, he rejoiced in these words: "It is my meditation all the day & more than my meat & drink to know how I shall make the saints of God to comprehend the visions that roll like an overflowing surge, before my mind."[2]

CHARLES: Wonderful, Rachel! We're diverging again, but so usefully! I suppose we would expect issues and circumstances to arise in which those things just discussed would be the focus of the trial of faith—not the Church's athletic program, for instance.

NOEL: I can surely agree, Charles. Particularly if our faith with regard to the Lord's plan of salvation is tried "in that thing." We might find ourselves dealing with suffering, loss of health or a loved one, worldliness, or feeling forsaken. It is less likely, and I presume this is the point you're making, Charles, that our faith would be tried in the abstract concerning the existence of the plan of salvation.

WINSTON: We are facing once again the reality that superficial devotion will not do. A moment or a circumstance will come, in one way or another, in which it will be shown whether or not we are true believers in the gospel of Jesus Christ!

RACHEL: It is to be hoped that in those circumstances we can be forgiven if, like that anxious father of the stricken young man about whom we have spoken, we too cry out, "Help thou mine unbelief." (Mark 9:24.)

NOEL: Painful as those moments may be, it is likewise true that we will receive, according to Moroni, a witness *after* the trial of our faith. (Ether 12:6.) Furthermore, through that trial our faith might be significantly strengthened. It might even, in some circumstances, move into the realm of knowledge!

CHARLES: Just as it is wise to make allowance for human imperfections in our association with other disciples, it is well to make allowance for irony and its role in human affairs. Sometimes the things we fear most are those that come upon us. So we must not automatically regard irony as a sign of God's disinterest. It is more a reflection of His precision.

Indeed, irony has unusual capacity to shape and mold us as the even flow of things could never do. Think of the athlete who is paralyzed; the usually perceptive person being "blind-sided" by something he especially should have been able to see coming; a doctor dying of the disease he has sought valiantly to cure.

PAULINE: Charles, may I say how much tonight has helped me to see that, if we know the fundamental truths, then we can trust the Lord in the midst of tactical perplexities. (1 Nephi 11:17.) Therefore, we should not repress the fact that we know that God loves us!

We all remember the words in the book of Alma about the instance of a busy, prestigious man who had been preoccupied with the cares of the world but who finally "owned up." Amulek said, "Nevertheless, after all this, I never have known much of the ways of the Lord, and his mysteries and marvelous power. I said I never had known much of these things; but behold, I mistake, for I have seen much of his mysteries and his marvelous power; yea, even in the preservation of the lives of this people. Nevertheless, I did harden my heart, for I was called many times and I would not hear; therefore I knew concerning these

things, yet I would not know; therefore I went on rebelling against God." (Alma 10:5, 6.)

NOEL: There is a third example in the scriptures concerning a group who had been baptized by fire and by
the Holy Ghost but who knew it not. (3 Nephi 9:20.)
Unaware of the spiritual gift they had been given,
perhaps it went unused and undeveloped.

CHARLES: It can be so with each of us. We can know
more than we are willing to acknowledge. We can also
fail to live up to our gifts and to our privileges. We can
even get mixed up and spend all our time trying to
cope with tactical perplexities without realizing, like
Amulek, that we *do* know. Hence, we can rely upon
the fundamentals—such as that God loves His children—even if we can't explain the meaning of what is
swirling about us at the moment. (1 Nephi 11:17.)
    Finally, as to the cares of the world and the things
of the world, it seems that if our hearts are so set upon
the things of this world, they must be broken before
they can be set upon the things of God—this, in order,
as Ezekiel urged, to "make you a new heart." (Ezekiel
18:31.)

PAULINE: We musn't forget Saul. His heart was also
changed! Give me a moment to find the words in
Samuel: "The Spirit of the Lord will come upon thee,
and thou shalt prophesy with them, and shalt be
turned into another man. . . . And it was so, that
when he had turned his back to go from Samuel, God
gave him another heart: and all those signs came to
pass that day." (1 Samuel 10:6, 9.)

JEFFREY: Pauline is truly one of those sister scripto-
rians about whom President Kimball spoke!

CHARLES: Let's take time after diverging, but useful diverging even so, for attempting summation. How else could we learn to choose except by passing through these clinical experiences, including those with regard to the cares, goods, and things of this world? As usual, there are several gospel principles to be balanced, sentinel scriptures that form the parameters of principles. First, from Timothy; then from the Doctrine and Covenants: "If any provide not for his own, and specially for those of his own house, he hath denied the faith, and is worse than an infidel." (1 Timothy 5:8.)

"Every man who is obliged to provide for his own family, let him provide, and he shall in nowise lose his crown; and let him labor in the Church." (D&C 75:28.)

JEFFREY: And—forgive the self-serving—even as to how we manage money: "Ye have sown much, and bring in little; ye eat, but ye have not enough; ye drink, but ye are not filled with drink; ye clothe you, but there is none warm; and he that earneth wages earneth wages to *put it into a bag with holes.*" (Haggai 1:6, italics added.)

Some of my clients have wondered about the "holes" in my investment plans for them . . .

CHARLES: Not I, Jeffrey. On another side of that square, we are warned, however, that it is easier for a camel to enter the eye of a needle than for a rich man to enter the kingdom of heaven. (Matthew 19:24.) Another and third parameter, however, is given us in the Book of Mormon: if having found Christ, we seek riches in order to do good, then such is acceptable. "Before ye seek for riches, seek ye for the kingdom of God. And *after* ye have obtained a hope in Christ ye shall obtain riches, if ye seek them; and ye will seek them for the intent to do good—to clothe the naked, and to feed the hungry, and to liberate the captive, and administer relief to the sick and the afflicted." (Jacob 2:18-19, italics added.)

NOEL: I'm glad Charles supplied that scripture. Such an effort at enrichment, however, is to be undertaken *after* individuals have first found Christ!

Another principle is found in the counsel Jesus gave to his apostles; therefore, this may not apply equally to everyone. (See 3 Nephi 13:25-34.) He said: "Take . . . no thought for the morrow: for the morrow shall take thought for the things of itself. Sufficient unto the day is the evil thereof." (Matthew 6:34.)

"He said unto his disciples, Therefore I say unto you, Take no thought for your life, what ye shall eat; neither for the body, what ye shall put on." (Luke 12:22.)

"Take ye no thought for the morrow, for what ye shall eat, or what ye shall drink, or wherewithal ye shall be clothed. For, consider the lilies of the field, how they grow, they toil not, neither do they spin; and the kingdoms of the world, in all their glory, are not arrayed like one of these. For your Father, who is in heaven, knoweth that you have need of all these things. Therefore, let the morrow take thought for the things of itself. Neither take ye thought beforehand what ye shall say; but treasure up in your minds continually the words of life, and it shall be given you in the very hour that portion that shall be meted unto every man." (D&C 84:81-85.)

CHARLES: Thank you, Noel. Thus we see how there are parameters and principles within which we are to stay. To be indifferent to the economic needs of our family would be wrong. To become too preoccupied with the things of the world would be equally dangerous. First things—even when we seek riches in order to help build the kingdom of God!

WINSTON: But within these parameters and principles, there is clearly ample opportunity for us to exercise our agency with regard to material things. If we get too close to one of the gospel guardrails, it can push us back.

But some other principles operate too. We are to impart of our substance to the poor without being too judgmental. (See Mosiah 4:17, 21, 26.) Yet we are responsible to help in a way that is truly helpful without condescension, without creating dependency relationships, and certainly "not to please ourselves." (Romans 15:1.) As an anxious governmental leader, I ponder this problem often!

PAULINE: Yes, it is all so very difficult to do, especially day by day.

CHARLES: It surely is! We cannot do it at all if we stray outside these guiding principles. But Pauline is right: making the day-to-day decisions even within those guiding principles is not always easy.

JEFFREY: Furthermore, urban living and governmental programs complicate the matter. These can depersonalize aid and appear to relieve us of individual responsibility for the disadvantaged.

CHARLES: Time to wind things up, I'm afraid. We'll all need our rest so we can be fresh tomorrow to readdress the cares of the world!

# Eighth Conversation: Spiritual Submissiveness

> " . . . And becometh as a child, submissive,
> meek, humble, patient, full of love, willing
> to submit to all things which the Lord
> seeth fit to inflict upon him, even as a child
> doth submit to his father."
> (Mosiah 3:19.)

*The setting: A summer evening in the home of Winston. All are present except Rachel, who is seriously ill in the hospital and whose grave condition has just been discussed in the group. The lesson is focused on a fundamental ingredient of true discipleship, spiritual submissiveness, and on the deep trust and faith submissiveness requires.*

---

WINSTON: Noel, thanks for the report on Rachel. I must say your presence tonight is especially appreciated in view of Rachel's sudden and very serious illness.

NOEL: As I reported, she's sleeping now. Besides, she wanted me to be here. It was all somewhat sudden, yet at our late spring get-together, Rachel knew something was wrong, as tests that very day had shown. Some of you may even have sensed it in her comments then. Anyway, I'm so grateful to be here. Please go ahead. I'll stay as long as I can before returning to the hospital.

In any event, the topic you've asked us to come prepared to discuss—true conversion and spiritual submissiveness—could not be more relevant or needed by me now. Rachel's actually doing much better than I am. She is more submissive, but even for her, submissiveness requires such deep trust.

WINSTON: Thank you, Noel. We will go ahead as planned, hoping for whatever comments you may choose to make.

Our lesson does concern a matter on which it is difficult to speak but impossible to remain silent. The presentation is not made in alarm but in genuine concern: Too few of us, as Church members, are genuinely and seriously involved in the process of becoming fully converted, which includes the submissiveness Noel described.

NOEL: And, Winston, you are not speaking of an absentee audience, but of ourselves!

PAULINE: Oh, yes! I agree with Noel. Each of us should say, "Lord, is it I?" (Matthew 26:22.)

WINSTON: So true, Pauline! Being more "anxiously engaged" in this process of conversion will be especially vital in our time as Church members feel the heat of both history and prophecy in convergence.

Full conversion includes but is much more than

Church activity and attendance. Its resulting righteousness is reflected in one's private as well as public behavior—in thoughts as well as in deeds. It means actually turning fully to God and fully away from the world—with objective and observable changes in one's life. Then, both beliefs and behavior testify to the transforming power of gospel truths. (See 2 Corinthians 3:15, 16.)

PAULINE  Again I so agree! While conversion does not produce instant perfection, it certainly reflects a resolute commitment to walk, with lengthened and quickened stride, the stretching path to perfection.

WINSTON: Yes. Without such full conversion, outwardly, one may be merely going through the motions, superficially participating in Church programs but being, nevertheless, comparatively untouched, unconverted, and unchanged inwardly.

NOEL:  As in baptism, so in Church activity—there can be immersion without conversion!

WINSTON:  Because of this sad reality, the Church is and must be much more than a mere transit lounge; it is to help, specifically and constantly, in the transforming of lives, in the perfecting of the Saints, in the teaching of doctrines, and in the administering of ordinances. Programs and activities are useful and provide much-needed and important scaffolding, but they are not the emerging structure itself. Therefore, what can be said about full conversion that might help us all? Jeffrey, your and Pauline's portion of the assignment please!

JEFFREY: All right, Winston. Whether cumulative or dramatic, the ingredients of the process of full conversion are the same. First, if we have not fully forsaken our sins, to that same degree, we are not fully underway. The Lord has said, "Return unto me, and repent of your sins, and be converted." (3 Nephi 9:13.)

When Paul commended members in Corinth, he did not exult over some lesser development in their lives, but he rejoiced because, wrote Paul, "Ye sorrowed after a godly sort, what carefulness it wrought in you, yea, what clearing of yourselves, yea, what indignation, yea, what fear, yea, what vehement desire, yea, what zeal, yea, what revenge! In all things ye have approved yourselves to be clear in this matter." (2 Corinthians 7:11.)

PAULINE: Second, forsaking our sins makes possible our serious pursuit of the demanding developmental process that is necessary in order to keep the Savior's breathtaking commandment to strive to become "even as I am." (3 Nephi 27:27; see also Matthew 5:48; 3 Nephi 12:48.) Our full acceptance of Christ thus includes the sobering commitment to strive to become more like Him!

JEFFREY: Third, full conversion includes becoming as a little child: "Verily I say unto you, Except ye be converted, and become as little children, ye shall not enter into the kingdom of heaven." (Matthew 18:3.) These words are more than nice imagery; they constitute a call to an incredible adventure, for, indeed, a true Saint, according to King Benjamin and Paul, "becometh as a child, submissive, meek, humble, patient, full of love, willing to submit to all things which the Lord seeth fit to inflict upon him, even as a child doth submit to his father." (Mosiah 3:19; see 2 Corinthians 5:17.)

PAULINE: Such full conversion, with its attendant child-likeness that Jeffrey just read about, was later required of even the chief apostle: "I have prayed for thee, that thy faith fail not: and when thou art converted, strengthen thy brethren." (Luke 22:32.) Note that Jesus spoke positively to Peter concerning "when," not "if," he was converted. One vital sign, therefore, that measures the degree of one's conversion is his degree of spiritual submissiveness. (See Matthew 18:4; 3 Nephi 9:22; 11:37, 38; Mosiah 3:19.)

JEFFREY: Submissiveness replaces selfishness, and meekness replaces pride, enabling the Lord to lead us along, taking account of our capacity and of our yet partial understanding of the great blessings that await the faithful. (See D&C 50:40; 61:36; 78:17.)

NOEL: But to underwrite such true conversion, clearly there must occur a "mighty"—not minor—"change" in one's heart, mustn't there? At least so many prophets, such as King Benjamin, Alma, Ezekiel, and Ammon, have so declared. For instance, "Cast away from you all your transgressions, . . . and make you a new heart and a new spirit." (Ezekiel 18:31.) Also, "When Ammon arose he . . . did . . . declare . . . that their hearts had been changed." (Alma 19:33.) It's there in Samuel's anointing of Saul, too. (See 1 Samuel 10.)

As I have come to love and appreciate Rachel more and more, I have seen how her even more complete conversion has brought about in her even more gentleness and graciousness amid a coarsening world. Just as King Benjamin said, "Ye will not have a mind to injure one another, but to live peaceably, and to render to every man according to that which is his due." (Mosiah 4:13.)

JEFFREY: Noel, you have surely described the Rachel we all know and love. No wonder when one prophet inquired of Church members, he did not ask about the statistics pertaining to a particular program; instead, Alma asked, "I ask of you, my brethren of the church, . . . Have ye experienced this mighty change in your hearts?" (Alma 5:14.)

WINSTON: Thank you Noel, Pauline, and Jeffrey! Achieving full conversion, as just presented, is no small task. Though there is often a crucial moment of belief and commitment, subsequent full conversion is not accomplished in an instant. Unsought for, it usually will be unexperienced. Moreover, partially converted members will not become, as Peter and Paul prescribed, sufficiently "grounded" and "rooted." (Ephesians 3:17; Colossians 1:23; 1 Peter 5:10.) Those with shallow root systems will be toppled by high winds or will be scorched and withered by heat from the sun of circumstance. (Matthew 13: 1-23; Alma 32: 37-40.)

The directive and illustrative words of the Lord to His early apostles in this dispensation are reminiscent of His earlier words to Peter. These words constitute solemn indicators of the soul-stretching nature of true conversion. Hence, as Pauline observed of Peter, there can be no exceptions, including the Twelve. (D&C 112:12, 13.)

NOEL: Yet, Winston, full conversion with its attending spiritual submissiveness may not occur until the individual has successfully passed through temptation and "much tribulation." (D&C 112:13.) It makes the soul shiver, doesn't it?

WINSTON: Hmmm. Indeed. The personal and developmental dimensions of conversion *are* soberingly specific! Yet, we live in a time in which far too many Church members are dimming rather than trimming their lamps. Trimming, by the way, means "to prepare for efficient burning," a state of readiness. Among the most sad words in all of scripture are those of the foolish virgins who lamented, "Our lamps are going out." (Matthew 25:8, alternate rendering of Greek.) Today, the lamps of some Church members, alas, "are going out" needlessly.

PAULINE: I agree! Instead, we are to "shine forth" (D&C 115:5), giving evidence of our genuine spiritual activity and submissiveness with that discernible radiance emanating from those who are converted, who become commandment-keepers, as with Lamoni: "Lamoni was under the power of God; . . . the dark veil of unbelief was being cast away from his mind, and the light which did light up his mind, which was the light of the glory of God, which was a marvelous light of his goodness—yea, this light had infused such joy into his soul, the cloud of darkness having been dispelled, and that the light of everlasting life was lit up in his soul." (Alma 19:6.)

CHARLES: How such illumination is needed today, especially amid humdrum hedonism and the spreading shadow of sensuous secularism!

WINSTON: So true, Charles. Hence the surprising amount of boredom among gross sinners. In obvious recognition of the constant and powerful pull of the world, those in process of full conversion are given counsel not to be "weary in well-doing." (Galatians 6:9; D&C 64:33.) This divine encouragement keeps us moving forward and carrying our crosses daily. (Luke

9:23.) It can also give us patience amid the injustices and incongruities in the world, as we discussed last time.

CHARLES: And even the added capacity to cope with our enemies. The only way that our enemies can finally be overcome is by love. The gospel of Jesus Christ does so much for us with regard to our enemies, doesn't it? For instance, it fixes their real identity as our spiritual brothers and sisters, children of the same Father in heaven. The Christian response to one's enemies is not only spiritual but also practical.

Still, it surely does not make the loving of one's enemy easy by any means. At least not for me! But it gives to us a framework of understanding and the motivation to try and to persist. Furthermore, this objective assumes a timeless significance in our lives.

WINSTON: If, however, we regard people only as functions, then they become something to be used, to be pushed out of the way, or even to be gotten rid of. Then people become inconveniences or even "enemies," or are responded to, at best, as in reciprocal honor among thieves.

JEFFREY: As we talk, it seems important to note that when one's conversion is full, one is also anchored in a base of valid, personal spiritual experiences. Jacob wrote: "He had hoped to shake me from the faith, notwithstanding the many revelations and the many things which I had seen concerning these things; for I truly had seen angels, and they had ministered unto me. And also, I had heard the voice of the Lord speaking unto me in very word, from time to time; wherefore, I could not be shaken." (Jacob 7:5.)

WINSTON: Even when someone is keeping the commandments, he may yet lack a particular dimension of spiritual submissiveness. (See Mark 10:17-22.) Past spiritual experiences can help us face our remaining spiritual deficiencies.

As Jesus Himself observed, if a son asked for bread, would a loving father give him a stone? (Matthew 7:9; Luke 11:11.) God's goodness is true not only in terms of our physical nourishment but also in terms of our needed spiritual growth. If we need a certain experience, a loving Father will not give us another—in spite of our pleadings! But initially there is milk before meat. As Paul wrote, "I have fed you with milk, and not with meat: for hitherto ye were not able to bear it, neither yet now are ye able." (1 Corinthians 3:2.)

NOEL: Well said, Winston. Hence, the Savior asks more of His followers than that they simply acknowledge Him. Otherwise, why would he say, "One thing thou lackest" or these words? Listen: "Be ye therefore perfect, even as your Father in heaven is perfect." (Matthew 5:48.)

"Therefore I would that ye should be perfect even as I, or your Father who is in heaven is perfect." (3 Nephi 12:48.)

"And know ye that ye shall be judges of this people, according to the judgment which I shall give unto you, which shall be just. Therefore, what manner of men ought ye to be? Verily I say unto you, even as I am." (3 Nephi 27:27.)

Jesus is completely serious about our need to grow individually by following Him and striving to become like Him. Thus, the most geniune form of *adoration* of Jesus is to be expressed by our *emulation* of Jesus. If not so, then why the marvelous episode concerning the rich, righteous young man we've discussed so often? (Mark 10:17-22.) Highly individualized challenges do come to each of us. I've pondered, especially the last few days, how the intensity of certain mortal learning experiences may be explainable only in terms of the interplay of working on present deficiencies in order to prepare for future opportunities, possibilities we now view only through a "glass darkly." I'm especially grateful now for our earlier discussions of these matters.

WINSTON: I feel the same way, Noel. You and Rachel have helped teach me so much, and you were so comforting when I became a widower!

So, in what zones of daily living might we expect to encounter the individualized things yet to be achieved in order to facilitate our full conversion?

CHARLES: Most likely, Winston, in those tendencies to be overcome and those sins yet to be fully forsaken—sins that, until cast off, will make us aliens in the kingdom of God—to which, therefore, we do not yet truly and fully belong!

PAULINE: Every sin—such as pride, anger, sloth, avarice, lust, and envy—inevitably causes a violation of God's two major commandments on which all the other laws and prophets hang. (Matthew 22:35-40; see D&C 42:29; John 14:15.) And, as we have been warned, the devil knocks at every door in the hotel of the heart until he finds one that is unlocked or ajar.

JEFFREY: Exactly. Sins are strikingly interactive. The proud are too haughty to love God with all of their hearts. Likewise, insufficient love of God leads to taking God's name in vain and to breaking the Sabbath day He has made for man. And the angry can scarcely love their neighbor, nor can those who envy or lust or who are filled with avarice and greed.

CHARLES: And, Jeffrey, those who are angry are more apt to lie, to covet, and, sadly, even to kill.

WINSTON: Those who are filled with lust will not only commit mental adultery but may commit actual adultery, fornication, or other things just as bad that are "like unto it." (D&C 59:6.)

PAULINE: Pride, too, is surely present in all our sins, whether in being too proud to honor one's father and mother or in being too concerned with preserving one's image to tell the truth. Or in breaching the ninth commandment by lying or by bearing false witness. By the way, Winston, you're becoming a veritable scriptorian of late!

WINSTON: These assignments do help! But frankly, it also seems that the Spirit has quickened my memories of the scriptures, memories that have lain latent for so many years!

NOEL: It surely seems so to me, Winston. Happily, the virtues such as love, meekness, faith, patience, and submissiveness are interactive too! Moroni said, "The first fruits of repentance is baptism; and baptism cometh by faith unto the fulfilling the commandments; and the fulfilling the commandments bringeth remission of sins; and the remission of sins bringeth meekness, and lowliness of heart; and because of meekness and lowliness of heart cometh the visitation of the Holy Ghost, which Comforter filleth with hope and perfect love, which love endureth by diligence unto prayer, until the end shall come, when all the saints shall dwell with God." (Moroni 8:25, 26.)

Paul declared, "In Jesus Christ neither circumcision availeth any thing, nor uncircumcision; but faith which worketh by love." (Galatians 5:66.) The scriptures also tell us that without meekness it is impossible to have faith. (See Moroni 7:43, 44.)

CHARLES: As you mention meekness, Noel, it seems there actually are some truths to be accepted meekly and by faith or not at all. But these are the very truths that appear to the world to be foolishness. (1 Corinthians 1:18, 23.) The Athenians, for instance, mocked Paul when he told them of the resurrection. (Acts 17:32.)

WINSTON: So true, Charles! Meekness does run grindingly against the grain of intellectual pride. For some, bending the knee is difficult, but less so than bending the mind.

CHARLES: When we kneel to pray, Winston, the head is last to incline.

WINSTON: Thank you for that apt and succinct comment.

Now, I'm afraid Pauline's compliment will make me self-conscious as I cite further scriptures, but here we go anyway!

Prestigious Amulek surely has his modern counterparts, as his words suggest an attitude we see all about us today: "I was called many times and I would not hear; therefore I knew concerning these things, yet I would not know; therefore I went on rebelling against God." (Alma 10:6.) Hopefully his modern counterparts will develop Amulek's intellectual honesty and humility!

NOEL: What C. S. Lewis says about "only two kinds of people" fits with spiritual submissiveness, doesn't it?

CHARLES: You mean, Noel, "There are only two kinds of people in the end: those who say to God, 'Thy will be done,' and those to whom God says, . . . '*Thy* will be done.'"[1]

NOEL: That is the one, Charles. And by way of reassurance, as we move through the process of conversion, falling short at times of full compliance, happily the Lord gives his glorious gifts to "those who love me and keep all my commandments, *and him that seeketh so to do.*" (D&C 46:9, italics added.)

Those last seven words are so reassuring! Little wonder that we must go on striving to take up the cross daily "with all the energy of heart," moving toward that developmental point when, fully converted, we will be more like the Lord and be "filled" with God's love! (Moroni 7:48.)

JEFFREY: Are you saying, Noel, that even those with great faith must still take up the cross daily?

NOEL: *Especially* those!

JEFFREY: Faith, even knowledge, gives no immunity from tests. In fact, it has seemed to Pauline and me that God's star pupils seem to get the most tests.

NOEL: They are probably the most ready for graduate or postdoctoral studies. Yet Jesus' experience in Gethsemane caused Him to cry out, asking if it would be possible that the cup could pass from Him. (Matthew 26:39.) Later Jesus actually felt forsaken. (Matthew 27:46.) It was not, however, that Jesus' perception of reality had changed. At one height of His agony, He thus cried aloud as to whether that through which He had pass to pass was, finally, necessary. He reached out to the Father for help just as Peter on the wave-tossed sea had earlier reached out to Jesus. (Matthew 14:30.)

Perhaps, as you both once said, Charles and

Winston, what is being experienced in our own tiny Gethsemanes, in our own miniature Calvarys, on those personal promontories of our human experience, is that special form of loneliness that prepares us for a special togetherness as we draw closer to God. In these situations, the distractions of the moment fall away. The essence of the human experience is compressed into what is almost one single moment, perhaps so that one's eye can become single to God and His will.

Perhaps, too, it is only in such darkness and solitude that the light of the gospel is seen in its full illumination. Perhaps therein the final act of spiritual submissiveness occurs when we surrender to God fully, completely, and totally—something we could scarcely do in the merriment of recreation or in distractions of the marketplace.

JEFFREY: In view of what you have just said so eloquently and probingly, Noel, if we could only keep alongside our questions of today those questions we will ask ourselves later if we falter now: "Why didn't I trust the Lord more?" "Why was I so anxious in view of all His past blessings to me?" "Did not our hearts burn within us?"

WINSTON: A powerful point, Jeffrey. As Noel has indicated so tenderly and insightfully, God finds it easier to shape our souls when there is humility and meekness present even if it is brought upon us by events. Yet it is still better if we humble ourselves "because of the word." (Alma 32:14.)

JEFFREY: When pure humility is not possible, though, circumstantial humility can be useful. Sadly, the latter sometimes disappears as soon as the adverse circumstances disappear. We are truly slow to remember our God. (Helaman 12:5.)

PAULINE: Apparently it is equally vital for us to learn obedience not only because that quality will help to save our souls here, but perhaps also because of chores in the distant future, chores that will require of us that strict kind of obedience.

WINSTON: How else could we acquire that quality except through the relevant clinical experiences.

CHARLES: Obedience training is not just for puppies! Suppose, however, that each exception or immunity from a needed experience would give us fewer opportunities in the world to come? What kind of Father in heaven would He be if He granted all our petitions for relief if doing so meant indulging us, trading transitory present pain for future endless joy?

Suppose too that the world for which we are being prepared is one filled with such abundant blessings and beauties that we could become self-indulgent later if we were not now trained to be truly obedient?

And suppose that the next world is one in which we may exercise considerable power and dominion— hence the importance of our learning to use power and authority based upon the principles of righteousness. (D&C 121:36.)

If we are to be trusted with far more than we have ever been trusted with here, we must be trained for that trust now, lest we damage others in massive ways later. Suppose, too, that in our continuing education on the other side of the veil, intellectual humility is a necessity. Suppose our capacity for mercy and empathy is to be developed now in order for us to better understand the consequences of misused agency later on.

NOEL: Charles, you were eloquent—and especially helpful to me! All of these possibilities and many more may be indications of "things as they really will be." (Jacob 4:13.) No wonder the training here in this probationary state must be so intensive—and so customized!

PAULINE: One can certainly see even more meaning in Eve's inquiry. Many of us must have wondered the same thing about our moments of perplexing and hard choices in the little universes of our own experience. When life is particularly stress filled, we must remember that once, anciently, when the plan of salvation was unfolded, we shouted for joy. (Job 38:7.)

NOEL: For the present moment, I don't question our previous consent, but I wonder a bit what all the shouting was about!

JEFFREY: As you graciously helped us to understand in a previous discussion, Noel, a deepened understanding of the gospel permits us to see that life is not so much lineal as experiential. Living represents more than the mere passing of time. These clusters of experiences constitute curricular crucibles within which our souls can be shaped and refined by fiery trials. (1 Peter 4:12.)

WINSTON: There appears to be no other way to acquire or deepen or obtain certain Christ-like traits and talents than to pass through the relevant experiences. The need is present for our equivalent of a reminding rooster to crow as for Peter, who thought that he was more spiritually mature than he then was.

NOEL: Thank you all for your reminding comments. How grateful I am for these reassuring ground rules from the scriptures: "Behold, ye are little children and ye cannot bear all things now; ye must grow in grace and in the knowledge of the truth." (D&C 50:40.)

"Ye cannot bear all things now; nevertheless, be of good cheer, for I will lead you along. The kingdom is yours and the blessings thereof are yours, and the riches of eternity are yours." (D&C 78:18.)

"There hath no temptation taken you but such as is common to man: but God is faithful, who will not suffer you to be tempted above that ye are able; but will with the temptation also make a way to escape, that ye may be able to bear it." (1 Corinthians 10:13.)

CHARLES: There is a great and perhaps unexplored lesson in the statement of Jesus that He did nothing save that which He had seen the Father do, isn't there? (John 5:19; see John 8:28.) Lately, as I have increasingly pondered the atonement, I've often wondered if that earlier "view" Jesus had of His Exemplary Father was not an immense help to Jesus later when Jesus felt the full weight of the atonement.[2]

NOEL: Perhaps, so, Charles, especially at that moment when Jesus trod the winepress alone. (D&C 76:107.)

WINSTON: One day when we look back at our mortal experiences, we will see that the achievement of full conversion constituted an enormous emancipation! No more misreading and misusing this life. No more hedonism. No more being a drag on those within our circles of influence. Instead, we will look back and see such divine justice and divine design. While we are in the thick of it, of course, it is difficult to understand. Charles once called it the "murky middle." Listen to Moroni on this point: "I, Moroni, would speak somewhat concerning these things; I would show unto the world that faith is things which are hoped for and not seen; wherefore, dispute not because ye see not, for ye receive no witness until after the trial of your faith." (Ether 12:6)

NOEL: Paul, who should know, wrote similarly, "It is a fearful thing to fall into the hands of the living God." (Hebrews 10:31.) Perhaps Paul had this in mind when he spoke about how no present chastenings seem to be joyous. Instead, these are hard to bear, though they are a necessary part of the tutoring experience through which we are passing. (Hebrews 12:6-7.)

CHARLES: Perhaps, too, some of these chastenings may, in fact, represent a blessed chance to lay a firmer hold upon a principle of the gospel that, if grasped, can change us. Or it may represent a needed chance to refine and polish an already existing attribute.

NOEL: A final seminar, Charles, in suffering before graduation?

PAULINE: Whichever, these clinical experiences reflect the love and mercy of God even though, at the time, it may be hard for us to see it. We should ponder frequently the importance of this superb declaration: "I know that [God] loveth his children; nevertheless, I do not know the meaning of all things." (1 Nephi 11:17.)

*(Moments later the group is led in fervent prayer by Charles with special pleadings for Rachel.)*

# Ninth Conversation:
# The Fruit of Righteousness

"Now no chastening for the present seemeth to
be joyous, but grievous: nevertheless afterward
it yieldeth the peaceable fruit of righteousness
unto them which are exercised thereby."
(Hebrews 12:11.)

*The setting: All the friends are once again in the home of
Noel and Rachel. A weary and weakened but mending Rachel
is home from the hospital after a very serious illness. Noel has
not had time to prepare a lesson, yet he and Rachel invited the
group to come as scheduled. Thus, unlike other evenings,
this is an impromptu discussion. Visits, prayers, blessings,
and expressions of concern and love have occurred throughout Rachel's illness.*

RACHEL: The love, faith, and prayers of this group
have meant so much. You'll never know . . .

NOEL: We really felt your faith and prayers, even when hope seemed unjustified medically!

CHARLES: Oh, how we all prayed and hoped! In our discussions of faith over the last few months, I'm afraid we've been a little neglectful of and a little hard on hope—without meaning to be, of course. It, too, is a precious principle of the gospel.

By the way, one of the "great intellectual milestones" of C. S. Lewis's education was his sudden realization concerning hope. He wrote, "You cannot hope and also think about hoping at the same moment; for in hope we look to hope's object and we interrupt this by (so to speak) turning round to look at the hope itself. Of course the two activities can and do alternate with great rapidity; but they are distinct and incompatible. . . . In introspection we try to look 'inside ourselves' and see what is going on. But nearly everything that was going on a moment before is stopped by the very act of our turning to look at it."[1]

NOEL: Hope does sustain us, Charles, while an experience is underway; it surely did us in our experience, the significance of which we do not even now fully understand. (Ether 12:6.)

PAULINE: In any case, meeting the challenges of the day by using the perspectives of eternity is the task—something you have both done so well, Rachel and Noel!

NOEL: I truly thank all of you for your love and prayers! Interesting, isn't it, that our circumstances can suddenly change but that God's word never does? We can be tossed to and fro by circumstances, but we are anchored by His word. We can even resume relationships with others just where we left off, rejoicing, as did Alma, that they are "still [our] brethren in the Lord." (Alma 17:2.)

WINSTON: Even resume conversations almost without skipping a sentence, Rachel!

NOEL: We feel that way about this group of friends. Especially now. And, Winston, your empathy was special. It has not been any more loving but more knowing. The rest of you will understand, I'm sure. Winston's empathy as a widower had a special authenticity as I faced that same prospect.

WINSTON: How necessary it is for us to have hope in extremity. May we read together, silently, an example of such hope? I refer to Alma's miraculous conversion. Please turn to Alma 36:17-22.

*(All pause to read.)*

NOEL: Alma's soul cry, "O Jesus, thou Son of God," echoes with happiness found: "And oh, what joy." (Verse 20.) Joy replaced pain. Perspective replaced darkness.

PAULINE: Yes, and Alma apparently saw God, causing him to exclaim "My soul did long to be there." (Verse 22.)

CHARLES: The ultimate homesickness . . .

NOEL: True, Charles! How touching is his yearning and his use of the word *long*.

JEFFREY: Yet, as a young man, he actually persecuted the Church! Like Saul, he was converted dramatically. (Mosiah 27:11-37.) Then he succeeded his father as presiding high priest of the Church, becoming the custodian of the sacred scriptural records. Alma is a special example of how the gospel is a gospel of hope!

WINSTON: So true! As far as I can tell, his is a unique case study. He was elected to be the first judge of the people, and after eight years of serving in dual duties, governmental and spiritual, he felt the Church needed his full attention, so he gave up his governmental duties. He was not confused about what came first. This is especially intriguing to me.

JEFFREY: On the other hand, I'm especially impressed by the fact that Alma was not content to be a mere caretaker of the records and files! Instead, he pressed forward spiritually until he learned personally that the records over which he was custodian were, in fact, true. Because of the spirit of revelation that was in him, he came to know that the words spoken by his fathers were true. (Alma 5:47.)

WINSTON: Yet the knowledge he had gained for himself was spiritual; it was not of the carnal mind. (Alma 36:4, 5.) And throughout his preachings, there was a simple, spiritual refrain!

CHARLES: Yes. And it is the same refrain that appears time and time again! God has a plan for mortals. Jesus is our Redeemer. The resurrection and the judgment are sure realities. Therefore, repent and keep the commandments.

What you have been through, Rachel and Noel! So submissive throughout! Spiritual submissiveness actually enhances people, doesn't it? In fact, it appears to enlarge the soul.

NOEL: But "without hypocrisy." (D&C 121:42.) Suffering surely squeezes out the trivia. Moreover, as noted by us before, there appears to be no immunity from suffering. How often, kicking and screaming, we are pulled toward a blessing! In fact, Peter wrote of the *democracy* of human difficulties: "The same afflictions are accomplished in your brethren that are in the world." But then he wrote about the *aristocracy* of Saints: "But the God of all grace, who hath called us unto his eternal glory by Christ Jesus, after that ye have suffered a while, make you perfect, stablish, strengthen, settle you." (1 Peter 5:9, 10.)

CHARLES: There's that word *settled* again.

NOEL: Part of my recent settling, by the way, has occurred by applying the wisdom in Peter's urging us to cast our cares upon the Lord because he cares for us. (1 Peter 5:7.)

RACHEL: We really came to feel the serenity of surrender, knowing that after all that could be done, we were in the Lord's hands.

NOEL: More than ever before, I see now that what we must strive to become is what He wants us to become, not what we want. What He wants for us is what we would want for ourselves if we knew what He knows. Such obeying and yielding to the Supreme Intelligence is an act of high intelligence.

PAULINE: It seems that afflictions of mortality are to be endured by all disciples in one way or another, including the Brethren—even in the particularized meaning of that word in our day.

NOEL: By casting one's cares upon the Lord and by knowing He loves us—even when we cannot understand the meaning of all things that are happening about us or to us—we permit the Lord to strengthen us, to give us courage and perseverance.

I saw a sweet and strong Rachel overcome her natural fears of death. I saw her possessed of a serenity that I envied then as I do even now! I saw a silent certitude in which Rachel knew more than could be expressed. There is an eloquence in such muteness!

CHARLES: Noel, you too have been an inspiration to us all. Don't diminish your own example. Besides, it may be that secondary sufferers, as you just were, have the toughest lot after all!

WINSTON: From what you said, Rachel, though at the brink, your faith-filled view of eternity undoubtedly actually grew more clear each passing moment. Without such real faith, the loss of a loved one, as I learned firsthand, or the loss of health, the scorn of the world, or the deprivations of life, can blot out our view of reality just as a small cloud cover can blot the sun. But the sun is still there!

RACHEL: Indeed it is! But there is no use in pretending one can pass through such experiences without noticing them, is there? That would reflect deep insensitivity. Disdain for death, which merely reflects a disdain of life, does not reflect moral courage. It is when one wants so desperately, even unselfishly, to stay but becomes willing to go that true submissiveness takes over. If we can feel and absorb adversity and still not lose our sweetness and perspective . . .

NOEL: Of the true disciples, it can always be said, "They kept the faith and the faith kept them!"

RACHEL: While we did not prepare a lesson for tonight, Noel and I wanted to introduce a future topic. We've not done our homework, just enough to feel it would be instructive for us to pursue later. Noel, describe our idea, will you please?

NOEL: Rachel and I began to read the scriptures together once again this past week after her return from the hospital. We're in the New Testament. We were struck by the questions Jesus put to various individuals or groups. Notice, even as a lad, how laden with meaning and import His questions were. We wondered if, later on, we might have a full session on the questions of Jesus. Here is just a sample: "After three days they found him in the temple, sitting in the midst of the doctors, both hearing them, and asking them questions. And all that heard him were astonished at his understanding and answers. And when they saw him, they were amazed: and his mother said unto him, Son, why hast thou thus dealt with us? behold, thy father and I have sought thee sorrowing. And he said unto them, How is it that ye sought me? wist ye not that I must be about my Father's business?" (Luke 2:46-49.)

Deep as His love was for His mother, Mary, and for His stepfather, Joseph, the Savior took occasion to remind them of who His real Father was!

PAULINE: What you're proposing fits with these verses, if I can find them. . . . Here, in the Joseph Smith translation: "Jesus grew up with his brethren, and waxed strong, and waited upon the Lord for the time of his ministry to come. And he served under his father, and he spake not as other men, neither could he be taught; for he needed not that any man should teach him. And after many years, the hour of his ministry drew nigh. (Matthew 3:24-26, JST.)

NOEL: Yes! Charles and I rejoiced over those same words, months ago. Jesus "served under" his father Joseph "but needed not that any man should teach him." A wonderful insight that accounts for his unique brilliance that astonished those in the temple. Thanks, Pauline!

RACHEL: And there was the episode with the penny. Jesus' question was, "Whose is this image and super-scription?" Then came the great lesson on rendering to Caesar that which was Caesar's and to God the things that are God's. (Matthew 22:15-22.)

WINSTON: A marvelous teaching episode—especially since the Lord's people are to be in but not of the world. Certain accommodations need to be made. I'd be less than honest, however, if I did not say, as one whose adult life has been spent in governmental ser-vice—

NOEL: And your contribution has been significant, Winston.

WINSTON: I hope so. But what I intended to say was that I hope Caesar will not ask us to render too much!

CHARLES: I fear he will, Winston. Rachel and Noel, are you saying more than that Jesus' questions were a useful teaching device?

NOEL: I hope so, though they were surely always that. I guess Rachel and I were impressed that not only did Jesus use questions to teach and to make memor-able points, but also to provide opportunities and to make a record that would be clear.

RACHEL: That is it, to give people a chance to be intel-lectually honest. For instance, listen to this exchange from Matthew: "While the Pharisees were gathered together, Jesus asked them, saying, What think ye of Christ? whose son is he? They say unto him, The Son of David. He saith unto them, How then doth David in spirit call him Lord, saying, The Lord said unto my Lord, Sit thou on my right hand, till I make thine enemies thy footstool? If David then call him Lord, how is he his son? And no man was able to answer him a word, neither durst any man from that day forth ask him any more questions." (Matthew 22:41-46.)

Though the Pharisees did not use the opportunity, Jesus was using the scriptures to give them a chance to see that though His lineage was physically through David, He was Jehovah![2] There was mercy in this opportunity, though it went unused! It was not just an erudite exchange!

CHARLES: I see the point more clearly. Perhaps you could elaborate upon the similar question Christ put to his disciples . . . here it is . . . also in Matthew: "When Jesus came into the coasts of Caesarea Philippi, he asked his disciples, saying, Whom do men say that I the Son of man am? And they said, Some say that thou art John the Baptist: some, Elias; and others, Jeremias, or one of the prophets. He saith unto them, But whom say ye that I am? And Simon Peter answered and said, Thou art the Christ, the Son of the living God. And Jesus answered and said unto him, Blessed art thou, Simon Bar-jona: for flesh and blood hath not revealed it unto thee, but my Father which is in heaven." (Matthew 16:13-17.)

NOEL: The difference is that Jesus' interrogation gave an opportunity for a declaration, and Peter seized upon it! This episode, as Rachel and I talked about it, seemed also to give the Twelve a chance to distinguish between various conclusions others had reached concerning Christ's identity and the correct conclusion.

Jesus did not want erroneous or careless thinking

done by his trusted Twelve. For instance, He did not want them following Him because they thought He was Elias! It reflects the precision that the Lord wants from us intellectually and spiritually—right reasons as well as right answers and right conduct!

JEFFREY: Perhaps the time when Jesus took Peter, James, and John to Gethsemane is another? The weary apostles had fallen asleep during Jesus' great agony, and Jesus' question was a mild reproof: "What, could ye not watch with me one hour?" "Their eyes were heavy," however, and they had slumbered and were no doubt embarrassed. (Matthew 26:40, 43.) I've often wondered if that episode did not serve as a spur later in their ministries when they were alone, when their flesh was weak and weary but, because of the memory of this episode, they kept going!

NOEL: Yes, Jeffrey! Though they did not and could not answer Jesus' question that awful yet wonderful night, in a way, they answered with the rest of their lives!

WINSTON: Other questions, like the one to the grateful healed leper, "Where are the nine?" (Luke 17:17) seem to be more rhetorical teaching, don't they?

RACHEL: Some are. Except that the question to the woman taken in adultery, "Woman, where are those thine accusers? hath no man condemned thee?" gave her a chance for a response. Then came Jesus' great emancipating utterance, "Neither do I condemn thee: go, and sin no more." (John 8:10-11.) Inspired questions can create moments of spiritual truth and can serve as springboards to further understanding.

CHARLES: As I think of this matter, I'm brought back to Noel's point that Jesus did not like carelessness of any form—behavioral or intellectual. Remember his question about John the Baptist? He asked the multitude, "What went ye out into the wilderness to see? A reed shaken with the wind?" (Matthew 11:7.) This was not just rhetorical, because it pointed out Jesus' high regard for John the Baptist.

NOEL: But it also showed how this popular prophet, who was so stern and unyielding, was actually an Elias who came to prepare the people for that which was to come. (Matthew 11:14.) John the Baptist had not disappointed the expectations of those who went out to see him as a prophet. If the multitudes and religious leaders of the day had searched the scriptures concerning the Messiah, Jesus would not have disappointed their expectations either! But so many in that day had false expectations about the Messiah, and of course, Jesus would and could not conform to their expectations. There is anguish, if not understandable frustration, in Jesus' question, it seems to me.

PAULINE: Perhaps there is some of the same, too, in Christ's inquiry of leaders in the Americas. Remember that they had not written down the words of Samuel the Lamanite? (See 3 Nephi 23:8-13.) These were vital words about how Saints who were resurrected would appear unto many!

NOEL: Yes, Pauline, such a crucial part of the scriptural record, especially in a book that was to come forth in our time, a time when, as foreseen, many doubt the reality of the resurrection! (See Moses 7:62; 1 Corinthians 15:1-23.)

RACHEL: There's so much more to know and to explore, isn't there? So much more to be covered while "conversing about this Jesus Christ"—just as our sisters and brothers in the land of Bountiful did so long ago. (3 Nephi 11:1, 2.)

WINSTON: We are living in a time in which secularism is becoming more sweeping and more powerful and pervasive, when many deny the existence of moral absolutes. Someone wrote of how "modern society . . . lives in the twilight of the absolute."[3] Enter ethical relativism.

CHARLES: Then from saying everything is relative, it is behaviorally but a short, next step, Winston, to saying anything is permissible. First in the realm of so-called private morality and then as to public behavior.

However, the truths of the scriptures, garnered throughout the ages, give us something against which we can set the present—with all its goodness, its hopes, its follies, and its fears. Listen to my—no, to *our*—friend Lewis: "A man who has lived in many places is not likely to be deceived by the local errors of his native village: the scholar has lived in many times and is therefore in some degree immune from the great cataract of nonsense that pours from the press and the microphone of his own age."[4]

WINSTON: So true, Charles! Especially if we combine true scholarship and the fullness of the scriptures for added perspective. By the way, in my recent reading, I found that Joseph Smith apparently felt, on one occasion in Philadelphia, that Sidney Rigdon, while preaching, was too neglectful of the Book of Mormon. Parley P. Pratt related, "While visiting with brother Joseph in Philadelphia, a very large church was opened for him to preach in, and about three thousand people assembled to hear him. Brother [Sidney] Rigdon spoke first, and dwelt on the Gospel, illustrating his doctrine by the Bible. When he was through, brother Joseph arose like a lion about to roar; and being full of the Holy Ghost, spoke in great power, bearing testimony of the visions he had seen, the ministering of angels which he had enjoyed; and how he had found the plates of the Book of Mormon, and translated them by the gift and power of God. He commenced by saying: 'If nobody else had the courage to testify of so glorious a message from Heaven, and of the finding of so glorious a record, he felt to do it in justice to the people, and leave the event with God.' The entire congregation were astounded; electrified, as it were, and overwhelmed with the sense of the truth and power by which he spoke, and the wonders which he related. A lasting impression was made; many souls were gathered into the fold. And I bear witness, that he, by his faithful and powerful testimony, cleared his garments of their blood."[5]

NOEL: I'd not heard that. Sidney Rigdon's scholarship in the Book of Mormon was underdeveloped. It is an impressive testimony from Joseph. We are so rich in resources and so blessed by added books of scripture! (1 Nephi 13:39, 40.)

JEFFREY: Sidney Rigdon's name reminds us, doesn't it, of earlier defections? The times ahead may produce some real challenges—treachery and betrayals—both from within our ranks and from without.

CHARLES: As to "without," I wonder if there will be some Gamaliels in the Sanhedrin of secularism who will speak up in the interest of fair play? And will there be some Pilates—though administratively weary— who will worry about yielding to the feelings of modern mobs? It is already clear that members of the

Church are treated quite differently than if we were merely nonsmoking humanists!

WINSTON: Yes. Even though those who write about us cannot be expected to agree with us or even appreciate us, I just wish that they would be more accurate and perceptive.

NOEL: A Church leader I know has even said he's often wanted to call a press conference in order to respond to questions he wished he'd been asked—not easy questions at all, but searching, sincere questions that could lead to more than superficial understanding and reporting!

WINSTON: Hmmm. But such enlarged understanding is not likely to be achieved. Others are too caught up in stereotypes and the anxieties of the day to really notice, it seems to me, either the happy light of the gospel or the ominous and prophesied developments.

Which French king was it who, while standing upon the gallows, bemoaned his own failure to see the rising tide of revolution by saying something like "Why could I not see this thing coming; why did I not do something?"

RACHEL: The perspectives of the scriptures are so precious. Those who are too busy to smell the flowers and to notice the sunset are not likely to pay any attention to the leaves on the fig tree. (Matthew 24:32.) Those who are too caught up in the hustle and bustle of life's seasons are not likely to notice when summer is nigh!

CHARLES: I sometimes sit in testimony meetings and wonder if, when we rightly testify to the truthfulness of the gospel, we also appreciate how important it is! So many today regard Christianity as irrelevant or question whether there was a historical Jesus! Yet into this gathering darkness has come . . . well . . . it's better said by the Lord: "When the times of the Gentiles is come in, a light shall break forth among them that sit in darkness, and it shall be the fulness of my gospel." (D&C 45:28.)

WINSTON: And so much of that needed light has come from other books of scripture, establishing the truth of the blessed Bible, which so many today, as foreseen, also, unfortunately, question. (See 1 Nephi 13:39, 40.)

NOEL: Yes, so true, Winston! Critics of the Bible who, for instance, complain that the genealogy of Jesus is rendered differently in Matthew 1 and Luke 3 need to ponder the First Vision. The Father introduced Jesus with these words: *"This is My Beloved Son. Hear Him!"* (Joseph Smith—History 1:17.) What other genealogy is needed?

RACHEL: And how the same First Vision puts to flight concerns over the historical Jesus!

NOEL: Furthermore, the appearance of other resurrected beings in this dispensation verifies the reality of the resurrection—not only of Jesus, but others as well!

We are so rich in reassurances! Charles may be right: We fail to appreciate the importance of the message of the restored gospel!

PAULINE: Perhaps that is why the Lord told Oliver Cowdery not to "suppose that he can say enough in my cause." (D&C 24:10.) And the Twelve in this dispensation are told to declare "morning by morning; and day after day . . . ; and when the night cometh let not the inhabitants of the earth slumber." (D&C 112:5.)

CHARLES: Pauline, you're amazing! How does one sign up for your seminary class?

NOEL: Let us not forget, too, all those references as to how modern scriptures will play a "convincing" role as to Jesus Christ, at least "among as many as shall believe" the restored words of scripture. (See 1 Nephi 13:39; 2 Nephi 3:11; 2 Nephi 25:18; 2 Nephi 26:12; Mormon 5:12-15; Moses 1:41.)

WINSTON: Such "convincing" is so needed now! And it needs to happen "because of the word" in advance of that day and time when, in a most compelling circumstance, all shall kneel and confess that Jesus is the Christ.

NOEL: Well, dear friends, tonight, in a sense, we return to the words of Alma where we began so many months ago in our focus on Jesus and faith in Him and His words. Alma said, "Do ye not suppose that they are more blessed who truly humble themselves because of the word? . . . Blessed are they who humble themselves without being compelled to be humble; . . . [who] believeth in the word of God . . . without being . . . compelled to know, before they will believe." (Alma 32:14, 16.)

WINSTON: In that context, one can understand why the resurrected Jesus appeared to Peter instead of Pilate, to the Eleven instead of to the Sanhedrin, to Mary instead of Caiaphas.

NOEL: And earlier, why the Lord appeared to Moses instead of Pharaoh. And why, too, the Lord guided obedient and inspired wise men, and not Herod, to the Babe Jesus.

RACHEL: Or, further, why the Lord chose to reveal the fulness of His doctrines to Joseph Smith instead of President James Monroe in 1820.

WINSTON: Monroe had other doctrines in which he was more interested.

*(Light laughter.)*

By the way, may I have the group's permission to bring a special friend next time?

RACHEL: Named Norma?

WINSTON: Yes. She knows and loves you, Rachel!

CHARLES: Everybody loves Rachel!

RACHEL: I'm so pleased, Winston!

JEFFREY: One thing I would like to do sometime is to invite Winston to tell us more about his idea for a book. Winston is going to call his book *The Christian Computer*.

WINSTON: Yes, perhaps I ought to do that sometime! The book, which will probably never be written, would detail the spiritual evolution of a skeptical scientist. He would put a multitude of key scriptures into a computer with the hopes of showing how they contradicted each other. Of course, as he comes to see, just the opposite occurs.

In any event, at the book's climax, the custodian comes in late at night to check the lighted computer laboratory and finds the computer scientist in his laboratory kneeling in prayer and surrounded by sheaves of printouts, the outpouring correlation of which has finally overcome his skepticism.

Right now, however, the book is all plot and no pages!

CHARLES: I wish you would write it, Winston!

NOEL: "The time is far spent." Thank the Lord for the

manner in which this group supports each other in love and in truth! May I assume the host's prerogative of reading a closing scripture? I meant what I said about our friendship, which rests in both "love and truth." May our friendships—now and later—reflect this verse in the Doctrine and Covenants: "That which is of God is light; and he that receiveth light, and continueth in God, receiveth more light; and that light groweth brighter and brighter until the perfect day." (D&C 50:24; see also D&C 84:45.)

May we enjoy each other now but also anticipate distant reunions and resumptions that will be a part of that "perfect day."

# Notes

*First Conversation: Faith and Knowledge*

1. Harrington, *The Politics at God's Funeral*, p. 119.
2. As quoted by Malcolm Muggeridge in "The Great Liberal Death Wish," *Imprimis*, May 1979.
3. *Hymns*, no. 196.
4. Smith, *Lectures on Faith* 3:4.
5. Ehat and Cook, eds., *The Words of Joseph Smith*, pp. 194-97.
6. *Lectures on Faith* 6:4.
7. Pratt, "True Faith" 13.
8. Smith, comp., *Teachings of the Prophet Joseph Smith*, p. 247.
9. Wordsworth, *The Excursion*, Book IV.
10. Christensen, *C. S. Lewis on Scripture*, pp. 26, 27.

*Third Conversation: Eternal Assurances*

1. Harrington, p. 114.
2. Singer, "Sanctity of Life or Quality of Life?" *Pediatrics* 72, no. 1 (1983): 129.
3. Young, *Journal of Discourses* 9:279; referred to elsewhere in notes as *JD*.
4. Smith, *C. S. Lewis: Patches of God-light*, p. 71.
5. Cannon, *JD* 26:191, 192.
6. Woodruff, *JD* 13:157.
7. Smith, *Gospel Doctrine*, pp. 62, 63.
8. Clark, *Conference Report*, October 1936, p. 114.
9. *Church News*, February 3, 1962, p. 2.
10. Lee, *Decisions for Successful Living*, p. 144.

*Fourth Conversation: Attitudes toward Faith*

1. Young, *JD* 9:149.
2. *Teachings of Joseph Smith*, p. 67.
3. Young, *JD* 7:55.
4. Talmage, *Articles of Faith*, pp. 96, 97.
5. Ibid., p. 100.
6. Richards, *Conference Report*, October 1937, p. 36.
7. Packer, "Faith," *Improvement Era*, November 1968, p. 62.
8. McConkie, ed., *Doctrines of Salvation* 2:302, 303.

*Fifth Conversation: The Plan of Salvation*

1. Shakespeare, *As You Like It*, act 2, scene 7.
2. Emma Smith Papers, August 1, 1868 or 1869, p. 4.

### Sixth Conversation: Spiritual Knowledge

1. Lewis, ed., *George MacDonald: An Anthology*, p. 67.
2. Lewis, *The World's Last Night*, pp. 10, 11.
3. Young, *JD* 11:102, 103.
4. Ibid. 12:192.
5. Ibid. 7:158.
6. Ibid. 12:169.
7. Ibid. 1:234.
8. Ibid. 13:142, 143.
9. *Words of Joseph Smith*, p. 237.
10. Lewis, *The Problem of Pain*, p. 26.
11. Kilby, ed., *A Mind Awake*, p. 87.
12. Lewis, *Letters to Malcolm: Chiefly on Prayer*, pp. 52, 53.

### Seventh Conversation: Cares of the World

1. *Words of Joseph Smith*, p. 369.
2. Ibid., p. 196.

### Eighth Conversation: Spiritual Submissiveness

1. Lewis, *The Great Divorce*, p. 156.
2. Talmage, *Jesus the Christ*, p. 661.

### Ninth Conversation: The Fruit of Righteousness

1. Keefe, *C. S. Lewis: Speaker and Teacher*, p. 26.
2. See *Jesus the Christ*, p. 552.
3. Harrington, p. 114.
4. Lewis, *The Weight of Glory*, p. 51.
5. Pratt, *The Autobiography of Parley P. Pratt*, pp. 298, 299.

# Bibliography

Anderson, Richard Lloyd. *Understanding Paul*. Salt Lake City, Utah: Deseret Book Company, 1983.

Christensen, Michael J. *C. S. Lewis on Scripture*. Waco, Texas: Word Books, 1979.

Clark, J. Reuben. *Conference Report*, October 1936, pp. 111-15.

Ehat, Andrew F., and Lyndon W. Cook, eds. and comps. *The Words of Joseph Smith: The Contemporary Accounts of the Nauvoo Discourses of the Prophet Joseph*. Provo, Utah: Religious Studies Center, Brigham Young University, 1980.

Emma Smith Papers, August 1, 1868 or 1869.

Farrer, Austin. "The Christian Apologist." In *Light on C. S. Lewis*, edited by Jocelyn Gibb. London: Geoffrey Bles, 1965.

Harrington, Michael. *The Politics at God's Funeral*. New York: Holt, Rinehart and Winston, 1983.

*Hymns: The Church of Jesus Christ of Latter-day Saints*. Salt Lake City, Utah: Deseret Book Company, 1948. No. 196.

Jessee, Dean C., ed. and comp. *The Personal Writings of Joseph Smith*. Salt Lake City, Utah: Deseret Book Company, 1984.

*Journal of Discourses*. 26 vols. Liverpool: F. D. Richards and others, 1855–86.

Keefe, Carolyn. *C. S. Lewis: Speaker and Teacher*. Grand Rapids, Michigan: Zondervan Publishing House, 1971.

Kilby, Clyde S. *A Mind Awake: An Anthology of C. S. Lewis*. New York: Harcourt, Brace & World, Inc., 1968.

Kimball, Spencer W. *Faith Precedes the Miracle*. Salt Lake City, Utah: Deseret Book Company, 1972.

Lee, Harold B. *Decisions for Successful Living*. Salt Lake City, Utah: Deseret Book Company, 1973.

Lewis, C. S., ed. *George MacDonald: An Anthology*. New York: Macmillan Publishing Company, 1947.

Lewis, C. S. *Letters to Malcolm: Chiefly on Prayer*. New York: Harcourt, Brace & World, Inc., 1964.

Lewis, C. S. *The Great Divorce*. In *The Best of C. S. Lewis*. Washington, D.C.: Canon Press, 1969.

Lewis, C. S. *The Problem of Pain*. London: The Centenary Press, 1943.

Lewis, C. S. *The Weight of Glory and Other Addresses*. New York: Macmillan Publishing Company, 1949.

Lewis, C. S. *The World's Last Night*. New York: Harcourt Brace Jovanovich, 1960.

McConkie, Bruce R., ed. *Doctrines of Salvation: Sermons and Writings of Joseph Fielding Smith*. Salt Lake City, Utah: Bookcraft, 1955.

Meynell, Alice. "Christ in the Universe." In *Modern British Poetry*, edited by Louis Untermeyer. New York: Harcourt, Brace & World, Inc., 1962.

Muggeridge, Malcolm. "The Great Liberal Death Wish." *Imprimis* (Hillsdale College, Michigan), May 1979.

Packer, Boyd K. "Faith." *Improvement Era,* November 1968, pp. 60-63.

Pratt, Orson. "True Faith." In *A Compilation Containing the Lectures on Faith,* compiled by N. B. Lundwall. N.p., n.d.

Pratt, Parley P. *The Autobiography of Parley P. Pratt.* Salt Lake City: Deseret Book Company, 1938.

Richards, Stephen L. *Conference Report,* October 1937, pp. 34-40.

Singer, Peter. "Sanctity of Life or Quality of Life?" *Pediatrics* 72, no. 1 (1983): 128, 129.

Smith, Joseph, Jr. *Lectures on Faith.* In *A Compilation Containing the Lectures on Faith,* compiled by N. B. Lundwall. N.p., n.d.

Smith, Joseph F. *Gospel Doctrine.* Salt Lake City, Utah: Deseret Book Company, 1977.

Smith, Joseph Fielding, comp. *Teachings of the Prophet Joseph Smith.* Salt Lake City, Utah: Deseret Book Company, 1977.

Smith, Robert Houston. *C. S. Lewis: Patches of God-light.* Athens, Georgia: University of Georgia Press, 1971.

Talmage, James E. *Articles of Faith.* Rev. Salt Lake City, Utah: The Church of Jesus Christ of Latter-day Saints, 1924.

Talmage, James E. *Jesus the Christ.* Salt Lake City, Utah: Deseret Book, 1916.

Williams, Duncan. *Trousered Apes.* New Rochelle, New York: Arlington House, 1971.

Wordsworth, William. *The Excursion,* Book IV. In *Wordsworth: Poetical Works,* edited by Thomas Hutchinson. Oxford: Oxford University Press, 1904.

# *Index*